Created *for* Belonging

Understanding the Longing to Feel
Connected and to Whom

Robert B. Shaw Jr.

WESTBOW
PRESS®
A DIVISION OF THOMAS NELSON
& ZONDERVAN

This book is a work of non-fiction. Unless otherwise noted, the author and the publisher make no explicit guarantees as to the accuracy of the information contained in this book and in some cases, names of people and places have been altered to protect their privacy.

WestBow Press books may be ordered through booksellers or by contacting:

WestBow Press
A Division of Thomas Nelson & Zondervan
1663 Liberty Drive
Bloomington, IN 47403
www.westbowpress.com
844-714-3454

Scripture quotations taken from the New American Standard Bible® (NASB), Copyright © 1960, 1962, 1963, 1968, 1971, 1972, 1973, 1975, 1977, 1995 by The Lockman Foundation Used by permission.

Scripture taken from the King James Version of the Bible

ISBN: 978-1-9736-3343-3 (sc)
ISBN: 978-1-9736-3345-7 (hc)
ISBN: 978-1-9736-3344-0 (e)

Library of Congress Control Number: 2018907952

Print information available on the last page.

WestBow Press rev. date: 05/21/2024

Contents

Foreword

P erhaps our most important emotional need is to belong.
Certainly, nothing hurts us more than to feel judged, left out,
abandoned, or rejected. There are many such experiences including
being picked last on a grade school playground; not making a team,
a music group, or a drama production; not being invited to the "cool
kids" party; turned down for a dream date; not getting into the
college we wanted; not landing a job we sought; or not ending up
with the spouse we longed for. No matter the form, rejection can be
devastating to our soul.

We all long to feel loved, wanted, respected, appreciated, and
valued. We need to belong because we know deep down we were
created to be a part of something (and Someone) larger than ourselves.

Originally, our loving Creator designed us to be warmly and
wonderfully attached to Himself and others. Unfortunately, ever
since sin entered the world, we have subconsciously hidden from
love, isolated ourselves from connections, and attempted to live
independently of our basic needs for healthy, mature interactions
with others. We hide, play it safe, and hesitate to venture into new
relationships because we fear getting hurt again.

Our intrinsic need to belong creates in us a powerful emotional
hunger for relationships. However, because we have been sickened by
them, we reactively rationalize that starvation is preferable to being

poisoned again by the toxin of rejection, abuse, being neglected, or being abandoned.

Due to that fear, many people stuff themselves with emotional and relational junk food—such as blindly running after relationships in addictive, reoccurring cycles of codependency or hard-hearted and calloused pseudo-independence in an ill-fated attempt to deny their need for others—which is neither healthy nor fulfilling. These dysfunctional protective mechanisms always and ironically result in disappointment, disaffection, discouragement, disgrace, and eventually destruction.

Thankfully, what you hold in your hands is an excellent guide to understand how to heal from past relational wounds and learn how to wisely, safely, and healthfully form positive, ongoing attachments with others.

Dr. Shaw has superbly crafted this powerful resource to help us find meaningful acceptance and fulfilling attachments in our everyday relationships with others. Written from his unique perspective as a minister and a mental health professional, Bob's book is sound and solid biblically and clinically. *Created for Belonging* will help support, encourage, and lead readers into forming healthy interpersonal relationships from which they can successfully derive a meaningful sense of belonging.

Psychologically, our sense of personhood and identity is based on our attachments to others. Learning how to effectively belong as well as give others a meaningful sense of belonging will prevent lifetimes of misery and help create hopeful futures of spiritual connection, emotional security, and relational fulfillment. This wonderful tool will be a useful and reliable road map to assist you in navigating the journey to health, holiness, and hope.

Enter through the narrow gate; for the gate is wide and the way is broad that leads to destruction, and there are many who enter through it. For the gate is small and the way is narrow that leads to life, and there are few who find it. (Matt. 7:13-14)

Rev. Jared Pingleton, PsyD
Assemblies of God Pastor
Licensed Clinical Psychologist
Vice President of Professional Development, American Association of Christian Counselors

Introduction

I t is inevitable when we are with people we just met to be asked, "So what do you do for a living?" and "Where are you from?" The first question elicits answers dealing with our jobs or vocations, which often reflect who we are. The latter has everything to do with our hometown, where we were born, and even who our family members are as these factors also contribute to who we are.

As such conversation progress, we may feel good or bad about the memories that flash across our minds as we describe our origins. These feelings and thoughts bring us back to times that are familiar—positive for most people but negative for many others—and they may even bring a sense of longing for something we are missing.

The conversation becomes especially exciting when we meet someone from our neck of the woods and connect with him or her more than others in a gathering. Discussing neighborhoods, activities, schools, and other familiar aspects can be nostalgic. What we are experiencing is the sense of belonging—or the lack thereof. Memories of how we were once connected to people and places that meant something to us back when can provoke a longing to reconnect with them. To have a common history with someone, something, or someplace brings a sense of security and connectedness we often lack in our current fast-paced, cell phone dependent, social media focused, and constantly moving society.

Several questions have always gone unanswered: What is my purpose? Where do I belong? Where can I go to feel loved? These questions come from the human spirit because God put them there; He was supposed to provide the answers. These questions and many similar ones reflect the longings of the human soul.

I want to acknowledge and thank Dr. Terry Wardle and Dr. Ann Halley for their ministry and teaching on formational prayer. This book is the fifth in the series of six that address the human core longings—the longing to belong. The six core longings in this series are these.

- Significance—we all desire a sense of identity.
- Covering—we all desire a sense of safety especially in relationships.
- Purpose—we all desire to know why we are here on earth.
- Understanding—we desire to know and be known by others and God.
- Belonging—we want to know how and to whom we are connected.
- Love—we want to love and be loved, the foundation of the universe.

Having a sense of belonging ignites a powerful desire to excel, explore, and be creative. It also drives the desire to be in relationships, which can end up healthy and long lasting or unhealthy, sporadic, and abusive. The difference between these polar outcomes is how the sense of belonging was either nurtured or neglected.

The desire to be connected to someone or something can be encouraged by love, mentoring, impartation, affirmation, and acceptance. Rejection, the essential fear in all human beings, is the ultimate sense of not belonging. Those who experience rejection will resort to whatever they can to gain acceptance.

All human beings are motivated to avoid two things—pain and rejection; the sense of belonging has a way of eradicating both. Pain often comes because of broken or abusive relationships that send a message of rejection and cause pain. When a relationship is restored in a healthy, loving framework, healing can take place to relieve pain and bring meaningful connectedness.

Ultimately, we belong to God. He created us. He loves us. He provided the world for our benefit. He wants us to be in relationship first and foremost with Him and then with one another. He created us in His image; if we truly examine ourselves, we realize we cannot find any other way to discover our ultimate meaning and connectedness outside of being connected ultimately to God.

Sin separates; that's why God hates sin. He is a relational God, and He hates sin because it separates us from Him. When brokenness, pain, and separation occurred due to Adam and Eve's rebellion, God set out to restore us to Himself. He chose a people to be the conduit for His presence in the world. Through Israel, He sent the Messiah, Jesus, through whom all people can return to a sense of belonging to Him.

Psychology reveals to us the need in every human being to feel connected and significant; without those qualities, people's ability to thrive is hampered or may not occur at all. Most theorists over the centuries have concluded that without a sense of purpose, positive regard (significance and love), belonging, and security, we develop dysfunctional ways to experience life, God, and others. Frankl, Maslow, Rogers, and Bowlby to name a few, have provided some legitimate insights into the human condition and need for connectedness. Though most theorists operated from a godless perspective, psychology still reveals aspects of the human condition that need addressing and ultimately redemption. Coupled with

God's Word and the transforming power of the Holy Spirit, we can experience some life-giving truths about our need for belonging.

I invite you to read this book, which will help you discover and perhaps rediscover your sense of belonging to something significant. I have dedicated a book to each of our core longings, but you will find that all of them are related and equally important.

The desire for belonging and love (see my book *Created for Love*) are perhaps the two core longings that seem to tie these all together. As we explore the sense of belonging, I believe you will find ways to understand yourself and others, gain a sense of identity and significance, see purpose emerge, and experience love and acceptance.

CHAPTER 1

A Sense of Belonging—
The Warm and Fuzzy of It All

We cannot live for ourselves alone. Our lives are connected by a thousand invisible threads, and along these sympathetic fibers, our actions run as causes and return to us as results.

—Herman Melville

Christians often report that turning to their bond with a loving God helps them deal with distress. They find comfort in their sense of belonging with and to God.

—Dr. Sue Johnson

I enjoy running. I was a high school and college middle-distance runner. Now, running is more of a therapy—part of my self-care—but I still like to compete in races from time to time. I run in parks, along the beach on vacation, and around neighborhoods.

Some time ago after moving to a new community, I measured a

three-mile course by driving my car around the neighborhood and checking my odometer to estimate the length. As I ran, I saw cars drive by and people doing yard work. We exchanged waves though we did not know each other, but we were all in the neighborhood, and I became a familiar face to them.

I became aware of a warm feeling when these people greeted me and I liked being acknowledged. It made me feel welcomed and a part of their neighborhood though they did not know who I was. It gave me a sense of belonging to the community that motivated me to be friendly in return and take pride in and protect the neighborhood I felt a part of.

Studies have suggested that a sense of recognition and belonging can deter individuals from causing harm in retail stores. For example, in partnership with the National Retail Federation and ADT Security, retail-loss expert Dr. Richard Hollinger of the University of Florida Department of Criminology, Law, and Society, revealed the results of the National Retail Security Survey over the summer or 2008 (Tanker 2008). He offered some general shoplifting prevention techniques: staying alert at all times, greeting all customers, and asking lingering customers if they need help.

I spent almost ten years as the manager of a retail store that sold Christian books, music, art, and gift items. We were consistently reminded in our training that we were not exempt from shoplifting or harm simply because we were a Christian bookstore. We were taught to simply acknowledge everyone who came in and to periodically check in with them while they shopped, and that did several things. First, it allowed me to acknowledge customers coming in. Second, it helped customers feel welcomed—as if they belonged. Finally, greeting customers acknowledged them and let them know they were no longer strangers to the store.

Of course, the more the customers knew they had been noticed and perhaps were being watched, the chances of them stealing something or doing harm were diminished. The positive aspect for most customers was that they got a sense of belonging, and those who may have been bent on shoplifting something were I'm sure in many cases, dissuaded from that which was a bonus. A sense of belonging is a powerful, positive feeling that meets a core longing in everyone.

Allow me to define belonging. According to psychologists, the need to belong is an intrinsic motivation to affiliate with others and be socially accepted. This need plays a role in a number of social phenomena such as self-presentation, self-esteem, a sense of identity, social comparison, acceptance, security, a sense of purpose, and an overall sense of community. Our need to belong drives us to seek stable, long-lasting relationships with others. It also motivates us to participate in social activities—clubs, sports teams, fan clubs, religious groups, and community organizations among them. By belonging to a group, we feel we are a part of something bigger and more important than ourselves. We all have such a desire. However, our need to belong can also lead to bad relationships and associations because our need to feel accepted and connected is very strong.

The need to belong runs deep. The biggest fear in most if not all human beings is the fear of rejection. Even though the core longings I have been writing about in this series exist in all human beings and are interrelated, perhaps by discussing the sense of belonging, we are able to see more clearly how our longings are pieces of a whole. When we know we belong, our desire for identity, security, purpose, and understanding seem somewhat fulfilled as well. We can't know ourselves by ourselves; being alone isn't good. Even God declared that truth from the beginning of the human race as he observed Adam: "It is not good for man to be alone" (Gen. 2:18).

Self-Focus

Humanistic psychology has a pervasive impact on counseling, education, child-rearing, and management with its emphasis on a positive self-concept, empathy, and the thought that people are basically good and can improve. By the 1960s, psychologists had become discontent with Freud's negativity and the mechanistic psychology of the behaviorists. Humanistic psychologists instead emphasized human potential. Abraham Maslow (1908–1970), an American psychologist and one of the pioneers of humanistic thinking, proposed that we as individuals were motivated by a hierarchy of needs. Beginning with physiological needs, we tried to reach the state of self-actualization—fulfilling our potential.

In 1943, Maslow developed what he called the hierarchy of needs. In his view, there were five levels of human needs that built on the previous level of needs. Maslow thought that people could not move up a level until their needs on the previous level had been met. While most other psychological theories at the time including psychoanalysis and behaviorism tended to focus on problematic and dysfunctional thinking and behavior, Maslow helped pioneer a new consideration. He was much more interested in learning more about what made people happy and what they did to become happy. He was more interested in what people did—good or bad—to obtain their basic needs. According to Maslow, self-actualization was the ultimate goal. Unfortunately, some eventually used his theory to develop what we now know as humanism and existentialism, which became unbalanced with their overemphasis on individualism and personal happiness.

The sense of belonging is part of one of Maslow's major needs that motivated human behavior. The hierarchy is usually portrayed as a pyramid with essential needs—food, water, air, sleep, shelter—at the base and more-complex needs—personal esteem and feelings of accomplishment—at the peak. The need for love and belonging lie at the middle of Maslow's pyramid as part of humans' social needs. While Maslow suggested these needs were less important than physiological and safety needs, he believed the need for belonging helped people experience companionship and acceptance through their relationships with family, friends, and others.

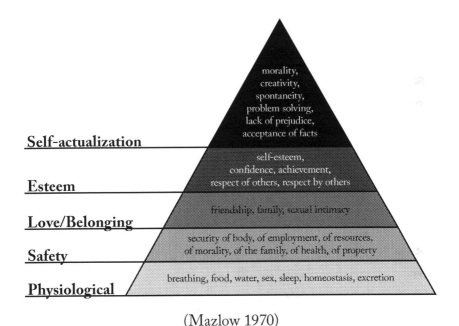

(Mazlow 1970)

Most research has not been able to substantiate Maslow's idea of a needs hierarchy and has found little evidence these needs are in a hierarchical order. Other criticisms of Maslow's theory note that his definition of self-actualization—the ultimate achievement for all individuals in his view—was difficult to test scientifically.

In addition, his research on self-actualization was also based on a very limited sample of individuals. The sample included people he knew as well as biographies of famous individuals Maslow believed to be self-actualized such as Albert Einstein and Eleanor Roosevelt (Cherry 2015).

Regardless of these criticisms, Maslow's hierarchy of needs represented part of an important shift in psychology. Rather than focusing on abnormal behavior and development, Maslow's humanistic psychology focused on the development of what he classified as healthy individuals (Cherry 2015).

While there was relatively little research supporting his theory, the concept of a hierarchy of needs became well known and popular in and outside psychology. In a 2011 study, University of Illinois researchers set out to put Maslow's hierarchy to the test and discovered that while fulfillment of the needs correlated strongly with happiness, people from cultures all over the world reported that self-actualization and social needs were important even when many of the most basic needs were unfulfilled (Cherry 2015). Essentially, the core longings of human beings relationally speaking—which include the sense of belonging—have no rank or priority; they are all equally important and interrelated. All people have the longings this book series addresses.

The sense of belonging is a powerful motivator of our behavior and the choices we make, but it is not any stronger or more important than the others—significance, safety, purpose, understanding, and love. All of these desires are equal in every human being; we all long to have them met. What may contribute to the pecking order of these innate desires are perhaps individual temperaments or personalities. Each individual may view a certain order depending on his or her qualifying views and needs, but we nonetheless all have these longings.

As a humanist, Maslow (and Carl Rogers, 1902–1987), believed people had an inborn desire to be self-actualized—to be all they could be (the US Army used a similar slogan to encourage individuals to enlist). A central feature of personality for Maslow and Rogers was the concept of self—all the thoughts and feelings we have in response to the question Who am I? They felt that a positive self-concept led to a positive worldview and a negative self-concept led to dissatisfaction and unhappiness. They and other were only partially correct; since Adam and Eve's rebellion, humans have had an innate desire to be self-oriented. Adam and Eve's first orientation was God-centered. After their rebellion in the Garden of Eden, sin became a growing experience in all humankind. Instead of being God-centered, humanity became self-centered. Humanism places human beings at the center of all things and makes them the measure of all things.

Rogers believed that we came with all the resources we would ever need prepackaged and that we simply needed to be on a path of self-discovery to extract what was already there. Christian psychologist Larry Crabb wrote,

> Carl Rogers, the major figure in the field of psychology who pioneered this line of thinking, is dangerously and heretically wrong. He offers acceptance without atonement and understanding rather than forgiveness. In his thinking, there is nothing terrible in us that requires forgiveness. The problem is *merely* disconnection, a state of detachment that is the result not of rebellious independence from God but of unfortunate psychological development. (Crabb 2005, p. 46)

However, instead of the "autonomous" being Rogers contemplated as the ideal product of counseling, the Bible teaches that humanity was made for God (Rev. 4:11) and dependent on Him (Acts 17:28).

In the current era, naturalism and the elevation of self have become embedded in Western culture. Maslow placed self-actualization as the highest need in his hierarchy of needs. God and neighbor are ignored or are afterthoughts, while self-fulfillment takes center stage. Personal experience becomes the "highest authority" in the person-centered counseling of Carl Rogers, and he was explicit in denying the ultimate authority of the Bible or God (Rogers 1961, p. 23–24). Paul Vitz called this modern humanistic psychology a religion, "a secular cult of the self" that rejected God and worshipped the self (Vitz 1994, p. xii). The effect of these theories has been to see the individual and the self as the primary focus in counseling. Counselors are directed to find ways to meet the needs of the self, to identify the inner strengths of the individual, to raise self-esteem, and to accommodate self-interest.

The biblical view does not deny the importance of the self. Rather, it opposes the idolatry of the self. In Genesis, Adam and Eve placed themselves above God by disobeying His will and in seeking guidance in life from another source of authority. Their fall into sin, evil, and the curse broke the bond in the relationship between humans and God. In response, God has provided the way of reconciliation (John 3:16, 14:6) through Christ, which requires a death to self and renewal and transformation in His Spirit.

Most if not all psychological theories remain self-oriented in their approach. In fact, most theorists have left God completely out of the human-development equation. Many approaches are even diametrically opposed to God at all levels. Some basic and legitimate criticisms of humanism are these.

- Concepts in humanistic psychology are vague and subjective and lack scientific basis.

- The individualism encouraged can lead to self-indulgence, selfishness, and an erosion of moral restraints.
- Humanistic psychology fails to appreciate the reality of our human capacity for evil.
- It lacks adequate balance between realistic optimism and despair.

God created human beings with various needs that were to be ultimately met by Him through relationship with Him; they were to experience fulfillment in Him and His presence. We have come a long way from God's intent. For thousands of years, human beings have sought to "find" themselves by themselves. We can all see how that has worked out.

Views of the self have changed over the centuries. The Old Testament Hebrews connected people to God, families, and community, and they would not have recognized the contemporary emphasis in our society on individual and personal rights. In America, the highest value is usually identified as individualism, which has infiltrated and has even been embraced by our church culture. We elevate the autonomous self. Secular theories of development describe the personality as moving through stages from dependence to independence and self-actualization. In contrast, the biblical model stresses mature personality development as moving from rebellion and selfishness to dependence on God and contributing to community—finding your place in the body of Christ.

Humanism is a distortion of what God has set in place. While humans are indeed the capstone of God's creation, we are all "actualized" when we are restored to relationship to God through the ministry, death, and resurrection of Jesus Christ. It is not because we have discovered we are the greatest on earth; rather, we realize our true, eternal value because God loved us enough to restore us to relationship with Him.

Without a restored relationship with God, we seek to meet our longings in our own power. If we are left to our own devices, our desire to belong will cause us to settle for, or simply fit in, or become linked with dangerous and unfulfilling people and situations. Can we actually belong to anything or anyone more meaningful than God, the Creator of the universe, and be considered part of His family?

At the other end of the relationship spectrum is codependency (more on that subject in chapter 4). As humanism takes a person away from deep, meaningful relationships into self-centeredness, codependency leads a person into deep, bondage-style relationships. Humanism lessens the importance of a sense of belonging; codependency is a relationship addiction. Codependence gives another person the power to give us meaning and identity. Essentially, it says, "I need you to need me." That is not just fitting in; that is losing oneself in another person. It appears to be and masquerades as a sense of belonging, but in reality it is bondage to another person.

Relationship Focused

Murray Bowen (1913–1990) was an American psychiatrist and professor of psychiatry at Georgetown University. Bowen was among the pioneers of family therapy, and in the 1950s, he developed a systems theory of the family. He believed that the interaction of family members was what developed into healthy or dysfunctional thinking and behavior. He coined the term *differentiation*—the ability to separate one's intellectual and emotional functioning from that of the family; a person can develop a sense of self but not at the expense of being in relationships. Individuals with low self-differentiation are more likely to become fused with predominant family member and emotions. Those with low self-differentiation depend on others' approval and acceptance. They either conform themselves to others in order to please them, or they attempt to force others to conform to them. As a result, they are more vulnerable to stress and "stress reactivity," and theirs is a greater than average challenge to adjust and adapt to life changes and contrary beliefs (Bowen 1974).

Those with generally "higher levels" of self-differentiation recognize that they need others, but they depend less on others' acceptance and approval. They do not merely adopt the attitude of those around them but acquire and maintain their principles thoughtfully. These principles, morals, and ethics help them to decide important family and social issues and to consciously or unconsciously resist lapsing into emotional reactivity and feelings-based (usually impulsive) thoughts and actions. They experience the benefit of community without the bondage to the group.

The practical application of this concept is the understanding that families are the most important environment in which we develop. Parents have perhaps the highest calling on earth—to raise children to be healthy and functional citizens. In fact, parents are not raising children; they are raising adults! How we interact (if at all) with one another in families has a dramatic effect on the way the next generation views themselves, others, and God.

Thus, despite conflict, criticism, and even rejection, those with a greater capacity to self-differentiate can stay calm and clear-headed enough to distinguish thinking rooted in a careful assessment of the facts from thinking clouded by emotion and their caving in to relationship pressures. Clear-thinking people are more-objective observers and more capable of calmness under relationship and task pressures. Paul wrote in Romans,

11

> For through the grace given to me I say to every man among you not to think more highly of himself than he ought to think; but to think so as to have sound judgment, as God has allotted to each a measure of faith. (Rom. 12:3)

Confident in their own thinking, such people can either support another's viewpoints without becoming wishy-washy, or they can reject another's opinions without becoming hostile to them or passively disconnected from them (Bowen 1974). Such people can disagree without the threat of feeling rejected or rejecting others.

Salvador Minuchin, a psychiatrist born in Argentina in 1921 and a contemporary of Bowen, was also a pioneer in the family systems approach to counseling. He along with contributions from Jay Haley (1923–2007) in California, developed what was called structured family therapy. Structural Family Therapy (or SFT) helps identify family interactions by identifying the organization of that family setting (Minuchin 1974). The primary assumption and foundation of this model is to identify family structure and the subsystems (child to male parent, child to female parent, child to child, etc.) that are formed through the level of authority and boundaries.

The objective was to understand how members of a family structure could learn to solve problems with a greater understanding of interactions (Nichols 2010). What is learned in the family setting has a great impact on how the family members relate to the world around them in various settings. According to Minuchin, a family was functional or dysfunctional based on its ability to adapt to various stressors within its subsystem boundaries (Seligman 2004).

In healthy families, parent-children boundaries are clear and allow parents to interact with some authority in negotiating between themselves the methods and goals of parenting. From the children's side, the parents are not enmeshed, overly dictatorial, or protective with the children, and that allows for healthy and positive sibling and peer interactions that produce socialization. But the parents are not so disengaged, rigid, or aloof that they ignore a child's need for support, nurture, protection, and guidance.

Dysfunctional families exhibit mixed and imbalanced subsystems and improper power hierarchies, for example, when an older child is brought into the parental subsystem to replace a physically or emotionally absent spouse. Another example is when a child is expected to be the emotional support for an adult parent. It is never appropriate for children to take on the role of an adult or parent since they are not emotionally or mentally equipped to do so.

I have found that what often develops is an understanding that to belong, someone must fulfill a role that was forced on him or her. In such cases, the feelings of belonging and acceptance hinge on being forced to please others at the expense of one's self-identity and well-being.

How we feel connected is critical in our development. Responsible parents prepare their children to be launched into adulthood. When parents hold back or neglect, abuse, discourage, overprotect, or fail to prepare their children that often leads to all kinds of dysfunction in the children, which can carry into adulthood. The balance is to impart to our children a sense of self but along with the skills to develop healthy relationships and know the importance of community. The healthy and biblical understanding is that we need God first and foremost, then each other; through one another, God helps develop individuals and their goals.

Young people are longing for connection, belonging, and meaning. Technology has often replaced the interpersonal relationship. Facebook and Twitter are just virtual worlds. Just because someone may have 783 friends on Facebook does not mean he or she has 783 friends in reality. Facebook may provide a superficial form of belonging and meaning, but ultimately, young people still long for something deeper, something greater. People may feel connected, but in reality, the connectedness is superficial and ultimately lacking. The growth of internet-based dating sites, profile-sharing sites, and ancestry sites are just some examples of the desire to truly connect with real, breathing, flesh-and-blood human beings even if it starts through an electronic site. Nothing can replace a real, honest-to-goodness, human-to-human, face-to-face, touch-to-touch relationship.

In reality, there is no sense of belonging in dysfunctional family scenarios but rather guilt, manipulation, and often a sense of failure. A sense of failure, for example, develops in the child and can last into adulthood mainly because someone with a sense of failure is not emotionally, mentally, or even physically equipped to be an adult in family dynamics if such a requirement is expected. Failing to be what they are forced to be when such a role is not possible leads to a sense of inadequacy, insecurity, and failure that lives on into adulthood. The sense of belonging, feeling a part of something as who they are, is altered because they are required to be who they are not to meet someone else's needs.

To focus only on self-actualization leads to a sense of entitlement, self-centeredness, reduced or nonexistent empathy, and pride. On the other hand, to be needy and dependent on someone else as a way to define who we are can lead to codependency, insecurity, and settling for what we don't want.

Ironically, I have found that if self-actualization is indeed the goal, individuals who pursue that are still lacking a sense of mental health because people cannot find themselves by themselves. The sense of belonging comprises healthy doses of both the ability to be in relationships and an understanding of how we know ourselves. Once again, God desires us to know who we are and to whom we are to be connected. In one approach, we may find ourselves, but for what purpose—to be only an island to one self? In the other approach, losing oneself in someone else (except Christ) or to a group is equally unfulfilling. One without the other leads to an imbalanced approach to self and relationship building.

God desires us to be restored to Him, sanctified, and at peace not simply for ourselves but so we can be in healthy relationships with Him and one another and make a positive impact in the world. As we allow God to satisfy our core longings, we learn to get along with others in more-healthy ways. To be in community and in fellowship is the essence of the kingdom of God. "The Center for Spiritual Development in Childhood and Adolescence has identified 'connecting and belonging' as a key theme for spiritual development" (Yust 2010, p. 292).

Spiritually, we all have fallen short of the glory of God (Rom. 3:23). Yet God reached out to us through Jesus and made it possible for us to be in relationship with Him again. Through Jesus's death and resurrection, we are reunited with our Father and belong to Him. We are loved by Him and understood by Him, and we find our identity in Him; we are secure in Him, and He gives us purpose. A sense of belonging has its benefits; it is essential for anyone's well-being, and knowing we belong to God brings ultimate benefits.

Chapter 2

Names Provide a Sense of Belonging

And there is salvation in no one else; for there is no
other name under heaven that has been given among men,
by which we must be saved.

—Acts 4:12

From when I was six until I was nine, my dad coached football
for a league comprised of teenagers who did not make their
high school football teams in an inner city of northern New Jersey.
Many of these teens were minorities who were not even given the
chance to try out for their high school football teams. These teams
were sponsored by various businesses in the city much like a little
league baseball program. These teams provided a sense of belonging
for these athletes and an opportunity to increase their confidence.
Many of the players made their high school football teams a year or
two after playing in this league.

I fondly remember my dad bringing me along with him to
practices and especially to games, and I had the exciting privilege of

roaming the sidelines with him. Coach Shaw was a well-liked and well-respected coach in this league, and for the most part, his players liked playing for him. What I remember embracing the most about being with my dad was how the players addressed me—most of them called me Little Shaw. I was identified with the Coach because of my last name and because of my relationship to him. I considered it an endearing moniker. Several of my dad's players would visit him after they had aged out of the league and especially after they returned from serving in the military during the Vietnam War since they knew my father was a World War II Marine combat veteran. Though I was in my early and mid-teens by that time, I was still Little Shaw to them; that provided me a sense of pride because of to whom I was connected.

All of us are connected by our names to someone. And there is always a lineage. In my case, since my dad was the youngest of four brothers, the Shaw boys were known in our community. They had an article written about them in the newspaper after the end of World War II because they had all served in the war (my uncles in the U.S. Army and my dad as a U.S. Marine), and they all returned home safely. One of my uncles was in the Battle of the Bulge in Europe, and my dad fought in the battles of Iwo Jima, Okinawa, and Midway. When my brother and I were born, the Shaw boys continued.

We grew up in postwar era in the inner city on a block that included mostly Scottish, Irish, and Italian families many of whom were immigrants, like my grandparents who came from Scotland in 1920. We had an awareness of ethnicity and our names. At that time, most of my friends and I were taught the importance of family, belonging, a sense of bringing honor to our name by our actions, and honoring our elders. Proverbs 22:1 says, "A good name is to be more desired than great riches, favor is better than silver and gold." When a sense of belonging is nurtured, it usually motivates us to give back and protect the community to which we feel connected.

All cultures place significance on names particularly last names. Surnames have historically been used to provide identity and a sense of belonging. In Scandinavian cultures, surnames can indicate to whom a child or family belongs; "Hanson" refers to the offspring as the "son of Hans" and "Bjornson" refers to the offspring as the "son of Bjorn." In the Jewish culture, names provided a prophetic meaning but also a sense of belonging. The name Bathsheba was not a formal name but rather a contracted name with a prefix "bath"; the name actually means "daughter of Sheba." In Matthew 16:17, Jesus said to Peter, "Blessed are you Simon Barjona." Barjona was not his last name. The prefix "bar" meant "son of" and described to whom Simon belonged. Jesus simply acknowledged that Simon was the son of Jonah. These examples affirm the identity given to the individuals. Jesus refers to James and John, two of His twelve disciples, as "sons of Zebedee" (Matt. 4:21; Luke 5:10).

When I look back through my own ancestry, my Scottish ancestors were named Robert, John, Alexander, Mary, and Thomas over several generations. James was a common name in my wife's lineage. These names seemed to have been family names given with meaning and familiarity and to perhaps honor another person in the family with the same name. We have decided to begin to name our children differently but with meaning. A few of the family names have become our sons' middle names, however. We named our oldest son Aaron, a Hebrew word meaning "high mountain," "exalted," or "enlightened." We named our next child Kenneth, a Scottish/Irish name meaning "handsome." We named our third son Jeremy, the English version of the Hebrew Jeremiah meaning "appointed by God." My wife gave our daughters names that helped describe them even from their date of birth. April Joy was indeed our month-of-April Joy. Bonnie Grace, which means "beautiful," is indeed beautiful. She was our fifth child, and five is the number for grace.

In the European cultures, last names, surnames, weren't widely used until after the Norman conquest in Europe in 1066. However, as the population grew in the various countries, people found it necessary to be more specific when they were talking about somebody else. As a result, people had to add certain descriptions of those they were discussing, which eventually lead to surnames. For example, descriptions like Thomas the Baker, Norman son of Richard, Henry the Whitehead, Elizabeth of the Field, and Joan of York ultimately developed into many of our current surnames. There are perhaps 45,000 different English surnames, but most had their origins from one of the following types.

In most cultures, tribal or clan names become the identifying characteristic. Scotland, Ireland, and England have clan names most of which came from an original patriarch or matriarch of the clan. These include Armstrong, Cameron, Campbell, Crawford, Douglas, Forbes, Grant, Henderson, Hunter, MacDonald, and Stewart. Patronymic surnames include Benson (the son of Ben), Davis (belonging to David), Dawson, Evans (belonging to Evan), Harris, Harrison (son of Harris), Jackson, Jones (Welsh for John), Nicholson, Richardson (son of Richard), Robinson, Rogers (belonging to Roger), Simpson, Stephenson, Thompson, Watson, and Wilson (son of Will). Matronymic surnames derived from female given names including Molson (from Moll, for Mary), Madison (from Maud), Emmott (from Emma), and Marriott (again from Mary).

Along with clan names, crests and symbols also became identifying components of the specific clans. There is the Shaw Clan with its crest; the McPherson Clan with its crest; the Buchanan

Clan with its crest, and the MacDonald Clan with its crest to name just a few. Incidentally, the prefix "Mac" or "Mc" means "son of," so MacDonald means "son of Donald" and MacPherson means "Son of Pherson." In Ireland, the prefix "O" as in O'Sullivan means "grandson of Sullivan."

In the German and Dutch cultures, the prefixes "von" and "van" mean "from"; Hans von Duisburg means Hans from the city of Duisburg. Vincent van Gogh was Vincent from the city of Gogh. Surnames also provided a clue for whom a servant worked. Someone named "Vickers" might have been a servant to someone named Vicker, and someone named Williams might either have served a William or been adopted by him.

Some surnames honored a patron. Hickman was Hick's man (Hick being a nickname for Richard). Kilpatrick was a follower of Patrick. These few cultural examples portray the importance of identity and a sense of belonging that is provided by the attachment to names most often a sense of belonging to a significant person like a parent, grandparent, or a community.

A last name may have pointed to where a person was born, lived, worked, or owned land. It might be from the name of a house, farm, hamlet, town, or county. Some examples are Bedford, Burton, Hamilton, Hampshire, and Sutton. The well-known writer Jack London had a stepfather who may have hailed from London. Those descended from landowners may have taken as their surname the name of their holdings, castle, manor, or estate such as Earle of Staunton. Windsor is a famous example — it was the surname King George V adopted for the British royal family. The famous American folk song writer and singer Henry John Deutschendorf Jr. adopted a city from his favorite state where he chose to live. He changed his surname accordingly and became John Denver (1943–1997).

Occupational names identified people based on their job or position in society. Calling a man "Thomas Carpenter" indicated that he worked with wood for a living, while someone named Knight bore a sword. Other occupational names include Archer, Baker, Brewer, Butcher, Carter, Clark, Cooper, Cook, Dyer, Farmer, Faulkner, Fisher, Fuller, Gardener, Glover, Head, Hunt or Hunter, Judge, Mason, Page, Parker, Potter, Sawyer, Slater, Smith, Taylor, Thatcher, Turner, Weaver, Woodman, and Wright (or variations such as Cartwright and Wainwright)—and there are many more.

Many names describe geographical features of the landscape from which a person came. Some examples are Bridge, Brooks, Bush, Camp, Fields, Forest, Greenwood, Grove, Hill, Knolles, Lake, Moore, Perry, Stone, Woods, and Woodruff. Author Margaret Atwood is probably descended from someone who lived "at the wood."

In medieval England before the time of professional theater, craft guilds put on mystery plays (mystery meaning "miracle"), which told Bible stories and had a call-and-response style of singing, perhaps being the origin of what is now liturgy used in many historical churches. A participant's surname such as King, Lord, Queen, Virgin, or Prophet may have reflected his or her role in the medieval productions, which some people played for life and passed down to their eldest son.

Some names, often adjectives, were based on nicknames that described a person. They may have described a person's size (Short, Long, Little), coloring (Black, White, Green, or Red, which could have evolved into "Reed"), or other character traits such as Stern, Strong, and Swift. Someone named Peacock might have been considered vain. This aspect of surnames or course is true of other languages and cultures all with the intent of attaching a sense of belonging and identity to someone.

In Asia, it is common for the surname to be listed first, often confusing others to believe it is a first name. Vietnam's former prime minister is Nguyen Tan Dung, and Nguyen is the most common surname in Vietnam—an estimated 40 percent of people in the country and the Vietnamese diaspora carry the name according to Vietnam's *Tuoi Tre News* and has its origin in the Chinese surname Ruan (Ghosh 2014), believed to be the name of a region in ancient China. The surname is popular because of the attachment to royalty, and many people in Vietnam have adopted the name to indicate attachment and loyalty to their rulers and ancestors.

In Japan, surnames are usually listed at the end of someone's name. The suffix "moto" means "base" or "origin"; the surname Hashimoto means "the base of a bridge" perhaps indicating where the family may have lived. Another example, the name, Nakahara means, "middle of a field" perhaps identifying where the family originated, where they lived, or where they were born.

In Africa, where there are over a thousand different ethnic groups, surnames can have multiple derivatives and meanings, but the sense of belonging to someone significant is often involved in the naming of children in these cultures. Many times, surnames are from tribal leaders, indicating a loyalty or a desire to ascribe royalty to a child or to a family. Other meanings of names relate to the place where a family lives, the day of the week a child was born, or a characteristic of God.

Church membership, which can create a sense of family, is another place that provides a sense of belonging. Individuals have identified themselves related to the church family to which they belong. For example, people may call themselves a Catholic, a Lutheran, a Methodist, or a Baptist to name just a few. While they are not formal surnames, such identifications attach people to a family of faith. Church membership, however, has been declining especially among the mainline denominations because many other options exist for individuals to join and from which to derive meaning.

In 2004, about 18.7 percent of the population attended church on Sundays, down from 20.4 percent in 1990 (Olsen 2004). Fifty years ago and more, families, churches, and neighborhoods provided a sense of belonging. More and more people are looking to fulfill this core longing through what the world has to offer, but that will eventually lead to disappointment or harm. "Cultures in rich societies are inciting people to an easy way of life. The values of wealth, power, and pleasure are seductive" (Vanier 2003, 166). The sense of community that underscores the sense of belonging has been diminished. As a result, we have experienced a decrease in the care for one another. Despite the trend, the sense of belonging remains a human core longing, which is simply not being met.

The basic question of this core longing is to whom or to what we belong. Adam belonged to God, and God belonged to Adam; that was established and was not in question after Adam was created. But the name Adam means "from the red earth." It was clear to Adam that he was the created, not the Creator. However, in addition, God knew Adam needed to relate to someone who was suitable for him and who was of like kind (Gen. 2:20). After naming all the animals, Adam evidently discovered he had no one like him with whom to relate. All humans are created and hardwired to be attached to someone and something. The accompanying result is often a sense of identity.

Adam's words after seeing Eve were poignant. Genesis 2:23–24 records Adam's reaction.

> And the man said, "This is now bone of my bones, and
> flesh of my flesh; She shall be called Woman, because she

was taken out of Man." For this cause a man shall leave his father and mother, and shall cleave to his wife; and they shall become one flesh.

Eve belonged to Adam and Adam belonged to Eve because they were totally connected through body, mind, and spirit; they were of like kind. Their identities were intricately compatible and connected to one another. They both ultimately belonged to God; their being was ultimately defined in God. The nature of God is equally reflected in both the man and the woman, which is why a marriage between a man and woman becomes the full expression through the oneness of both genders. However, they also felt a sense of belonging to each other. This was God's design for humankind in general and specifically men and women in marriage. This is the essence of family, which is the foundation of every human culture and relationship: to know where we belong and to whom.

According to Clinton and Sibcy (2006, p. 11), we internally ask questions that point to aspects of relationships, and how these questions are answered determines the connectedness we have with another person. For example:

- Are you there for me? Can I count on you?
- Do you really care about me?
- Am I worthy of your love and protection?
- What do I have to do to get your attention, your affection, your heart?

These questions and more are amplified during adolescence, and parents tend to have difficulty juggling discipline and connectedness. One study based on 12,118 adolescents from grades seven through twelve showed that these teens reported that connectedness with their parents topped the list of protective factors for the teenagers' health (Resnick et al. 1997). The report was consistent regardless of whether the teens lived in dual-parent or single-parent households. Teens who were in regular touch with their parents and felt valued by them were less likely to smoke, drink, or experiment with drugs and early sex according to Clarke and Dawson (1998).

Over the past few decades, who we are attached to and how that attachment manifests has been the study of many social scientists and psychologists. What they have discovered and how it promotes or detracts from the sense of belonging we all desire is the topic of the next chapter.

CHAPTER 3
Attachment and Belonging

If a community values its children it must cherish their parents.

—John Bowlby, 1951

For all who are being led by the Spirit of God, these are sons of God. For you have not received a spirit of slavery leading to fear again, but you have received a spirit of adoption as sons by which we cry out, "Abba! Father!"

—Romans 8:15

Veronica was a twenty-year-old college student who sought counseling because of symptoms of depression and a lack of direction in her life. She presented herself with a great deal of anguish about her life and lack of hope. As she discussed her background and life, it became quite apparent that she had never felt attached to her family or to anyone who had trustworthy staying power in her life.

Veronica was the fifth child of a career US military officer father

26

and a physician mother. One factor that contributed to her lack of attachment was the constant moving and relocating that is common among military service members and their families. On average, military families reside in one place for only about two to three years before they are required to move on to another military facility. As a result, the sense of belonging rarely takes place especially in youngsters, and that can leave them feeling isolated, alone, and even unloved. The lack of friends and extended family nearby can develop into a feeling of not belonging anywhere or to anyone. Such was the case with Veronica.

In addition, her feeling of detachment was exacerbated by the fact that her parents were in constant conflict, always angry, always yelling at each other, and never seemingly coming to a resolution. The constant conflict Veronica heard and witnessed caused feelings of insecurity, anger she kept internalized, a fear of a broken family, and self-doubt just to name a few of her problems. In addition, her parents' conflict often spilled over on her; she was demeaned, insulted, and verbally abused as well for no reason. "The bottom line is that our most intense feelings are tied to connections we make with the people we love or need the most" (Clinton and Sibcy 2006, p. 38). When the connections cannot be made with those we need the most as was the case with Veronica, a deep sense of detachment occurs and with it a longing for connection that is frustrated. When a youngster feels detached within the family, the ability to feel connected and to form relationships is hampered.

Veronica described herself as "floating" with no real sense of belonging, and she felt it was her fault that no one connected meaningfully with her. Because of the constant focus of conflict that occurred between her parents and the moving from one community to another due to her father's military career, Veronica never felt anyone was interested in her or her dreams and desires. She reported that she had had only one birthday party; therefore, she never felt she had ever been "celebrated." She expressed a lack of having anyone believe in her, and as a result, she felt invisible. The disconnect she felt caused her to feel her life was not important and no one would ever miss her if she were gone. Fortunately, she chose counseling and inner healing to help her realize that her life and dreams were important and that she was carrying undeserved guilt.

Belonging to another person has many variations and descriptions. There are several ways to describe people who are close to each other and seem compatible and at ease in their relationship. One example is when two people are so close emotionally that it is as if they were attached at the hip. They might be close in a business way too such as partners who work very closely. It can positively refer to any relationship in which two people function as if they were one.

The science of psychology addresses the longing to belong. Several theories and concepts have emerged in the field of psychology during the nineteenth and twentieth centuries that have contributed to the understanding of the importance of being attached to others. What has become known as attachment theory has morphed into a few offshoots that touch on the longing for belonging all humans possess.

One of the more fascinating aspects of the study of psychology is that all the theorists that have developed certain approaches to psychology and counseling had their own life-developing experiences and stories from which they derived their theories of human development. Some theories are demented and way off the mark because of their godless orientation, while others are helpful.

Sigmund Freud (1856–1939) based his theory of human development on his belief that all human stages simply stated came from inner appetites and sexual fantasies. He became jealous of his father, who was receiving attention from his mother, which he felt he himself should have been receiving. As an adult, he engaged in self-analysis of his dreams and childhood memories. His explorations of his feelings of hostility toward his father and rivalrous jealousy over his mother's affections led him to develop his theory of the origin of neuroses. As a result, he surmised that since he was sexually jealous of his mother's affection toward his father, it must be therefore true for all people to have repressed sexual fantasies that needed to be addressed. His attachment theory, if you will, was primarily based on sexual attachment.

The Swiss physician Jean Piaget (1896–1980) developed his theory of human development from being a loving and doting father to his two children. He intensely observed their tendencies and development as they grew up. As a result, he developed his four stages of human development separated by specific age categories because of what he saw in his children during those ages.

Another example is Viktor Frankl (1905–1997), who specialized in theories of depression, existentialism, suicide, and humanity's search for meaning. These approaches came from his imprisonment in and survival of Nazi concentration camps. His best-selling book *Man's Search for Meaning*, chronicled his experiences as a concentration camp inmate, which led him to discover the importance of finding meaning in all forms of existence even the most brutal ones and thus a reason to continue living. Frankl and his sister were the only survivors among his family members; his parents, brother, and wife died in the Nazi camps. His seemingly random survival of these horrible and traumatic experiences affected his view of the meaning of life, purpose, and relationships.

John Bowlby (1907–1990) also had a personal story from which he developed his psychological approach. He as well as others can say that how they experienced trauma, loss, and a broken sense of belonging helped him compile his belief system that developed into a psychological approach to human development and counseling. Along with others, he developed the theory of attachment.

Attachment

Attachment theory is a concept in developmental psychology that addresses the importance of attachment in regards to personal development as impacted by relationships throughout the early years of development. Specifically, it claims that the ability for an individual to form an emotional and physical attachment to another person gives a sense of stability and security necessary to take risks, branch out, and grow and develop as a personality (*Psychologist World* 2016).

As we understand it prominently today, attachment theory was developed by John Bowlby, who was born in London into an upper-middle-income family as the fourth of six children. The Bowlby family hired a nanny to be in charge of raising the children in a separate nursery in the house, and she had two nursemaids to help her raise the children. As a result, Bowlby was raised primarily by nursemaid Minnie, who acted as a mother figure to him and his siblings.

His father, Sir Anthony Bowlby, was a surgeon to the household of the king of England, and during World War I, he often left home to serve the king in the war. His father came home once or twice a year and had very little contact with him and his siblings. When Dr. Bowlby married Mary, they regularly experienced many months of separation. To resolve this prolonged separation, Mary decided to visit her husband for six months while leaving her firstborn daughter, Winnie, in the care of a nanny. This separation between Mary and her children became a common theme for all of their six children's lives as they were primarily raised by the nannies and nursemaids. Bowlby's mother received several letters while her husband, Anthony, was serving in the war. However, she did not share any of the letters with her children, and as a result, John Bowlby had no contact with his father. This was so impactful in Bowlby's childhood that it could have potentially influenced his key research focus on separation.

Normally, John Bowlby saw his mother only one hour a day after teatime, though during the summer, she was more available. Like many other mothers of her social class, she thought that parental attention and affection would lead to dangerous spoiling of the children. Bowlby was lucky in that the nanny in his family was present in his early childhood.

However, when Bowlby was almost four years old, his nursemaid and primary caretaker left the family. Bowlby was extremely affected by the loss of this caring individual, and later in life, he described this event as tragic as the loss of a mother. After his nursemaid left the family, Bowlby and his siblings were under the primary care of a nanny who was less than nurturing with Bowlby and his siblings due to her cold and sarcastic nature. This early loss of Bowlby's mother figure fueled his interest later in life around what became known as attachment theory.

When Bowlby was ten years old, he was sent to boarding school, which was common for boys of his social status. Bowlby's parents decided to send him and his older brother, Tony, off to the preparatory school to protect them from the bombing attacks due to the ongoing war. In his 1973 work *Separation: Anxiety and Anger*, Bowlby revealed that he regarded it as a terrible time for him.

In addition, Bowlby experienced the tragic loss of his beloved godfather during his childhood, which was another theme of separation and loss that could have contributed to his focus on separation research later in his career. During the first winter of World War II, Bowlby began working on his first published work *Forty-four Juvenile Thieves* that he published in 1944, close to the end of the war. Bowlby studied several children during his time at the Canonbury Clinic and developed a research project based on case studies of children's behaviors and family histories (Kanter 2007).

Bowlby examined forty-four delinquent children from Canonbury who had a history of stealing and compared them to "controls"—other children from Canonbury who were being treated for various reasons but did not have a history of stealing. One of Bowlby's main findings was that seventeen of the forty-four thieves had experienced early and prolonged separation (six months or more) from their primary caregivers before age five (Bowlby 1946). In comparison, only two out of the forty-four who did not steal had experienced prolonged separation from their primary caregivers before age five (Bowlby 1946). More specifically, Bowlby found that twelve out of the fourteen children who were categorized as "affectionless" were found to have experienced complete and prolonged separation before age five (Bowlby 1946). These findings were important and drew more attention to the impact of a child's early environmental experiences on their healthy development.

Later, Mary Ainsworth became a main contributor to Bowlby's work and theories, and together, they developed what we know today as attachment theory (Ainsworth and Bowlby 1991). Bowlby revolutionized our thinking about a child's tie to his or her mother and its disruption through separation, deprivation, or bereavement (Bretherton 1992). Mary Ainsworth contributed the concept of the attachment figure as a secure base from which an infant could explore the world, and she formulated the concept of maternal sensitivity to infant signals and its role in the development of infant-mother attachment patterns (Bretherton 1992).

Infants become attached to adults who are sensitive and responsive in social interactions with the infants and who remain as consistent caregivers for some months from about six months to age two. Parental responses lead to the development of patterns of attachment that in turn lead to internal working models that guide the individual's feelings, thoughts, and expectations in later relationships (Bretherton and Munholland 1999).

More specifically, Bowlby explained in his three-volume series on attachment (1973, 1980, and 1982) that all humans develop an internal working model of the self and an internal working model of others. The self-model and the other-model are built off early experiences with primary caregivers and shape expectations about future interactions with others and interactions in interpersonal relationships. The self-model will determine how individuals see themselves, which will impact their self-confidence, self-esteem, and dependency. The other model will determine how individuals see others, which will affect their avoidance-or-approach orientation, loneliness, isolation, and social interactions. In Bowlby's approach, infants are considered as needing a secure relationship with adult caregivers without which normal social and emotional development will not occur.

Bowlby's major conclusion was that to grow up mentally healthy, "the infant and young child should experience a warm, intimate, and continuous relationship with his mother (or permanent mother substitute) in which both find satisfaction and enjoyment" (Bowlby 1951, p. 13). He broke with psychoanalytic theories that saw infants' internal lives as being determined by fantasy rather than real-life events.

Bowlby and others proposed that children were born with an innate drive to form attachments with caregivers. He believed the earliest bonds formed by children with their caregivers had a critical impact that continued throughout life (Cherry 2016). Some critics profoundly disagreed with the necessity for maternal (or equivalent) love to function normally or that the formation of an ongoing relationship with a child was an important part of parenting (Rutter 1995).

Psychologists have proposed two main theories believed to be important in forming attachments. These theories are consistent with the historical debate on whether nature or nurture determines how each of us develops. Today, the debate has lessened some as many believe both nature and nurture affect human development and each influences the other.

The learning/behaviorist (nurture) theory of attachment suggests that attachment is a set of learned behaviors (McLeod 2009). The basis for the learning of attachments is the provision of food, which is directly related to Freud's concepts of human development. Infants will initially form attachments to whoever feeds them. They learn to associate the feeder (usually the mother) with the comfort of being fed, and through the process of classical conditioning, they find contact with the mother comforting. They also find that certain behaviors (e.g. crying, smiling) bring desirable responses from others (e.g. attention, comfort), and through the process of operant conditioning, they learn to repeat these behaviors to get whatever they want.

The more prominent theory of attachment, which Bowlby helped establish, suggests that children come into the world biologically preprogrammed to form attachments with others because that will help them survive (McLeod 2009). This understanding is definitely consistent with the fact that God created all of us for relationships and the longing we all have to belong to someone.

Infants develop innate social-releaser behaviors such as crying and smiling that stimulate innate caregiving responses from adults. The determinant of attachment is not food but care and responsiveness.

However, I believe nurture or its lack affects the natural desire to connect and attach. If the innate desire to belong is not met, is neglected, or is abused, the environment alters children's and adolescents' ability to sense belonging.

Bowlby suggested that a child would initially form only one primary attachment that acted as a secure base for exploring the world. The attachment relationship acts as a prototype for all future social relationships, so disrupting it can have severe consequences. This theory also suggests that there is a critical period for developing an attachment—birth to age five. If an attachment has not developed during this period, children will suffer irreversible developmental consequences such as reduced intelligence and increased aggression (McLeod 2009).

Bowlby's attachment theory stresses the following important tenets.

- Children between six months and thirty months are very likely to form emotional attachments to familiar caregivers especially if the adults are sensitive and responsive to child communications.
- The emotional attachments of young children are shown behaviorally in their preferences for particular familiar people, their tendency to seek proximity to those people especially in times of distress, and their ability to use the familiar adults as a secure base from which to explore the environment.
- The formation of emotional attachments contributes to the foundation of later emotional and personality development, and the type of behavior toward familiar adults shown by toddlers has some continuity with the social behaviors they will show later in life.

- Events that interfere with attachment such as abrupt separation of the toddler from familiar people or the significant inability of caregivers to be sensitive, responsive, or consistent in their interactions have short-term and possible long-term negative impacts on the child's emotional and cognitive life. (Mercer 2006)

Essentially, there are three keys points to Bowlby's observations according to Clinton and Sibcy (2006).

- If the significant person (mother) is sufficiently near, sensitive, and responsive, a child will feel secure, loved, and self-confident and will be playful, smiling, willing to explore, sociable, and show a basic sense of trust for self and others.
- If the significant person (mother) is not sufficiently near, sensitive, and responsive, a child will feel fearful and anxious. This develops into at least two types of defenses: avoidance (watchful, wary, and slow to trust) or ambivalence (alternating between angry and clingy, distrusting everyone).
- A fearful and anxious child will use relationship-seeking behaviors such as among others trying to make eye contact, pleading, or clinging. (Clinton and Sibcy 2006, p. 20)

The developing relationship style has one of two dimensions: a self-dimension and an others-dimension. The self-dimension centers around two critical questions:

- Am I worthy of being loved?
- Am I able to do what I need to do to get the love I need? (Clinton and Sibcy 2006).

The others-dimension is centered on its own critical questions:

- Are other people reliable and trustworthy?
- Are people accessible and willing to respond to me when I need them? (Clinton and Sibcy 2006).

How people answer these questions determines whether they have positive or negative views of themselves and their world. How youngsters answer these questions will determine the type of attachment style they will develop in adolescence as well as into adulthood unless healing of the inner wounds takes place.

The longing to belong as it manifests through childhood attachment experiences will be either somewhat satisfied or deficient. The deficient sense of belonging develops into an unhealthy and negative belief system and therefore into unhealthy behaviors several of which will be discussed in chapter 6.

Attachment Styles

Based on youngsters' attachment experiences, several styles of relationship constructs will develop in them—ways they may view relationships and the sense of belonging that encompasses them. Those who connect well with others exhibit certain characteristics of relationship building such as the ability to emotionally connect with others, the ability and freedom to disclose private thoughts and feelings, and the ability to participate in nonsexual touch (Clinton and Sibcy 2006).

It is generally understood that there are four attachment styles: ambivalent or fearful, disorganized or anxious, avoidant, and secure. According to Clinton and Sibcy (2006), they are distinguished as follows:

The ambivalent or fearful attachment people feel unloved and unwanted, are vulnerable to any perceived offense, have trouble trusting authority figures, can be needy and therefore drive people away, and lack confidence in their abilities to make life work. The beliefs that drive the ambivalent style are:

- I am not worthy of love.
- I am not capable of getting the love I need without being angry and clingy.
- Others are capable of meeting my needs but might not do so because of my flaws.
- Others can be trustworthy and reliable, but they might abandon me because of my worthlessness (Clinton and Sibcy 2006, p. 87)

This is an overview of the fearful attachment style:

Fearful people have a negative view of both their self and others, experience high levels of avoidance and anxiety, seek acceptance and self-worth from others, but fear that others are not capable of meeting their needs. These adults have a very difficult time with intimacy and closeness, and they often avoid relationships altogether. (Clinton and Straub 2010, p. 68)

The beliefs that influence the disorganized or anxious attachment style are these:

- I am not worthy of love.
- I am not capable of getting the love I need without being angry and clingy.
- Others are unable to meet my needs.
- Others are untrustworthy and unreliable.
- Others are abusive and I deserve it (Clinton and Sibcy 2006, p. 103)

This is an overview of the anxious attachment style:

> Anxious people hold to a negative view of their self and an unrealistically positive view of others. As a result, they are usually anxious in relationships are afraid of rejection, crave closeness, and are obsessively worried, needy, and clingy in their closest relationships. They have an unhealthy fear of abandonment because they believe that are not worthy of love. (Clinton and Straub 2010, p. 67–68)

Avoidant attachment people have difficulty with nonsexual touch. They have difficulty with emotional connections and often run from such aspects of relationships. They also do not readily share private thoughts and feelings with others. The beliefs that drive the avoidant attachment style are these.

- I am worthy of love based on my success and accomplishments.
- I am capable of receiving love, but I depend on my own self and abilities.
- Others are either unwilling or incapable of loving me.
- Others are not trustworthy; they are unreliable when it comes to meeting my needs (Clinton and Sibcy 2006, p. 67)

Here is an overview of the avoidant attachment style:

> Avoidant people are the opposite of anxious people, in that avoidants have an overly positive view of the self, but an excessive negative view of others. People who are avoidant are uncomfortable with closeness and tend to become overly self-reliant because they do not believe others will be there for them. (Clinton and Straub 2010, p. 68)

Finally, the secure attachment style, the healthiest style of the four, leads to positive relationship building skills and lifestyles. This attachment style describes those who hold a positive view of their self and others and are thus comfortable with closeness and independence (Clinton and Straub 2010). They take responsibility for themselves and find the courage to act when action is needed. The belief system that impacts this attachment style are: I am worthy of love, I am capable of getting the love and support I need, and others are willing and able to love me (Clinton and Sibcy 2006, p. 49).

This is an overview of the secure attachment style:

> Secure attachment describes those who hold a positive view of their self and others, experience feelings of positive self-worth, and have a healthy means of coping with stress. Because they believe that are worthy of love, and that others are capable and accessible when they need them, secure people are comfortable with both closeness and independence. (Clinton and Straub 2010, p. 67–68)

If you are interested in discovering your attachment style, refer to the survey in the appendix at the end of this book. Please note that your attachment style can change based on the level of a particular relationship or by the grace and healing power of God, who transforms minds, emotions, and perspectives through the impartation of His truth. I hope all of us know and experience the secure attachment style to fulfill the sense of belonging we all desire.

As an added perspective, two more resources emerged in the turbulent 1960s. The emotional upheaval, the desire to find oneself, the rock 'n' roll music culture, and the rise of popular psychology contributed to the need to find answers for one's life and relationships.

Fortunately, the rise of the Jesus movement was also occurring during this time. While many young people were becoming born again and accepting Christ as their Lord and Savior, many more were getting involved in open sex, drugs, and antiestablishment mentalities. Self-esteem was becoming a buzzword, and relationships were taking on new dimensions; as a result, the need for knowledge and understanding of the cultural dynamics of the times was increasing. Popular psychology was emerging to help provide answers.

One of the voices of those times was Dr. Eric Berne (1910–1970), who developed what he called Transactional Analysis, or TA. Transactional Analysis was essentially a repackaging of Bowlby's and Ainsworth's attachment theories. Berne suggested that people operated from at least three standpoints—they saw themselves as children, adults, or parents, and that affected the types of relationships they developed. People could experience certain dynamics in relationships based on the transaction between them and others.

- A child-to-child relationship—both parties are seeking self-centered fulfillments, have drama-filled communication, and experience over-emotionalism.

41

- A child-to-parent relationship—the "child" often feels inferior to the "parent" and will succumb to the parent's directives; the parent seeks to manipulate the "child."
- A child-to-adult relationship—similar to the above, but the adult is not always seeking to control the "child," but the "child" is still intimidated by the "adult" and tends to remain codependent on someone else.
- A parent-to-parent relationship—this dynamic brings constant conflict as both parties see themselves in control of the relationship and will not relinquish or submit to the other.
- A parent-to-adult relationship—similar to the above transaction in that there will be conflict, but the adult will often see things as they are and respond more positively at times.
- An adult-to-adult relationship—this is the most positive, healthy transaction as the two people can communicate on the same level, understand each other, experience a healthy give-and-take and mutual submission at appropriate times, and overall enjoy a good, satisfying relationship. The adult-to-adult relationship is the most mature and healthy interaction according to Berne.

One of Berne's followers was Dr. Thomas Harris (1910–1995). After a long career with the Navy, Harris entered private practice in Sacramento, California in 1956. Around this time, Dr. Eric Berne of Carmel was getting ready to publish his new theory on Transactional Analysis (TA). Dr. Harris went on to study with Dr. Berne and became a new breed of psychiatrist embracing the techniques of TA but with an attachment-theory view. After the phenomenal success of Berne's book *Games People Play* in 1964, Harris published his book,

I'm OK—You're OK in 1969. Harris's book was his slant on TA based on Berne's work.

After *I'm OK—You're OK*, Harris went on to become a director of the International Transactional Analysis Association. Dr. Harris served in the US Navy and survived the attack on Pearl Harbor. He went on to complete his medical degree at Temple University Medical School and rose to become the chief of psychiatry in the Department of the Navy. Dr. Harris continued with an active life in psychiatry and practitioner of TA.

In his best-selling book, Dr. Harris discussed four TA aspects, and as you read them, you will note the basic foundations of attachment theory.

- I'm okay, you're okay—equality and positive assessment of self and others
- I'm not okay, you're okay—self feels inferior to others
- I'm not okay, you're not okay—extreme pessimism with both self and others as inferior
- I'm okay, you're not okay—self feels superior to others

These aspects were presented as self-esteem issues and how self-esteem affects the way we perceive others and conduct relationships. Self-esteem is determined by how we relate to others and how they relate to us indicating that how we are connected to one another has a dramatic effect on how we view ourselves. Harris's view, however, leads us down the comparison mind-set that can be quite skewed. No matter how we compare ourselves to others, human nature tends to bring each of us to the short side of good self-esteem. In others words, can we ever view ourselves in a healthy way without comparing ourselves to others? The key is understanding and realizing how

God sees us as His beloved, redeemed, and empowered children and seeing ourselves as God sees us.

The sense of belonging is related to how people perceive themselves, their need for others, and how to connect in healthy ways. Connectedness, another way to describe belonging, will be discussed in the next chapter.

Chapter 4

Connectedness

Anyone who goes too far alone goes mad.

—Jewish proverb

The mass of men lead lives of quiet desperation.

—Henry David Thoreau

In the 2015 Star Wars movie *The Force Awakens* produced in 2015 by Lucasfilms, LTD, is a scene in which Rey, the main female character, speaks to BB-8, a droid robot who had been abandoned by its master.

REY: Don't give up hope. He still might show up—whoever it is you are waiting for. I know all about waiting.

BB-8: (*makes some electronic sounds as a question to Rey*)

REY: My family. They'll be back ... one day.

Rey's comment hints of a longing for an important relationship to be restored. We were created for relationships. God created us to be in relationship first with Him. Then He fashioned a woman to be with the man, Adam, to begin the family—the foundation of all life on earth. Once Eve came into Adam's life, Satan set out to wreak havoc on this foundation. Unfortunately, the devil was successful then, and he continues to be today. The center of all feelings of connectedness is the family. If the family is splintered, too often so will its members be.

Connectedness comprises two essential aspects: interactions with other people that are face-to-fact encounters including conversations and sharing, and a feeling of being cared about. Studies have shown that when connectedness is absent, a "failure to thrive" takes place. We may all get by without connection at least for a little while, but if we really want to thrive, we have to connect to each other (Schafler 2017).

For example, in orphanages where children are not helped, cuddled, or even touched, the failure to thrive is manifested by low birth weight, slow growth, and development, and they lag behind children who are cared for. One of the primary challenges faced by adopting parents is realizing their adopted children may have had altering attachment experiences prior to adoption. The result is often unmet expectations, which is a recurrent theme among couples who adopt children (Nehrbass, 2017). Some parents overestimate their ability to handle disappointed expectations. Nehrbass says:

> Realistic expectations will include knowing, understanding, and accepting the fact that marriage is hard, parenting is harder, and parenting adopted children is harder still. A realistic expectation is that the first year of an adoption of

a child over two years of age will be the most difficult year in their life. (Nehrbass, 2017, p. 370)

Adopting a child, while a loving and gracious thing to do, has its challenges. First the parents may not always know the full depth of the child's experience prior to adoption. Neglect, abuse, and other experiences will contribute to the challenges of attachment to the adopting parents. Some adopted children may have legitimate diagnosable mental health or developmental health conditions. There are spiritual dynamics as well since adopting parents may not know the spiritual or ritual abuse which may have occurred with the child prior to adoption. All of these contribute to the difficulty in the child's ability to connect and attach to the adopting parents and family.

As the child develops, an understanding that they were adopted may have mixed feelings—both a feeling of love and being wanted, but contrasted with feelings of abandonment and rejection. The parents may need extra efforts to help the child feel a sense of belonging. They may agree to an open adoption, where the child can choose to connect with their birth parents if they decide to do so, or a closed adoption where such an option is not usually possible. Whatever the case, adoption often involves loss, overcoming an absent sense of belonging, trauma, and tragedy. Be aware of the following types of grief:

- Child's loss of biological parents to death
- Child's loss of biological parents by court order (jail, incompetence, neglect, abuse)
- Child's loss of relationship with siblings
- Child's loss of cultural heritage (language, country, food, community)

- Child's loss of extended family (grandparents, aunts, and uncles)
- Child's loss of emotional or physical health, due to neglect or abuse in the past
- Losses in the adoptive parents' history that affect their ability to have healthy, attached relationships
- Adoptive parents' grief over infertility
- Adoptive parents' grief over unmet expectations (Nehrbass, 2017, p. 381)

Adopted children may experience mental health and spiritual issues such as, attachment disorders, depression, Attention Deficit Hyperactivity Disorder (ADHD), exposure to sexual trauma and therefore potential sexual disorders, potential future substance abuse, and behavioral disorders. The time it may take for an adopted child to feel a sense of belonging will vary, but it usually takes years until the child will feel connected.

Ultimately, the idea of adoption is mostly positive, as adopting parents are rescuing a child from an unstable, neglectful, or an abusive situation to a loving nurturing environment. The bible speaks of the spirit of adoption, stated in Romans 8:15, "For you have not received a spirit of slavery leading to fear again, but you have received a spirit of adoption as sons by which we cry out, 'Abba, Father!'" The word Abba, means "daddy" depicting the intimate nature of the relationship between the Father and His sons and daughters. A true sense of belonging has resulted from God's loving effort to bring us into His family. The spirit of adoption is simply rescuing someone from a negative experience and situation (sin and separation from God and each other; bringing a child to one's home from an orphanage or a foster home situation) and providing someone a positive loving environment, where connection and intimacy can occur. God does that through Jesus Christ, as Galatians 4:4-5 states:

> But when the fullness of the time came, God sent forth His Son, born of a woman, born under the Law, so that He might redeem those who were under the Law, that we might receive the adoption as sons.

Similar experiences of neglect and rejection can occur in the elderly population as well. Nursing homes and assisted living communities have exploded on our country's landscape and are places where older citizens can live among their peers, but often without the sense of feeling connected to family members. At any age, feeling alone, forgotten, devalued, unloved, and not being touched can lead to depression and can decrease the desire to live.

I know a family—I'll call them the Smiths—who have experienced a restoration of feeling connected and a sense of belonging. The couple currently has four young children with the oldest two being from the wife's previous marriage. In the wife's first marriage, the husband abandoned the family when the children were ages one and three, and he never remained engaged in the children's lives. The wife remarried after her divorce, and she and her second husband have had two children together. The husband, a strong family man, treated the first two children as his own from the very beginning, and they began to call him Daddy after a year into the marriage.

As the two older children became absorbed and accepted into their stepfather's family, they began to feel they belonged to their stepfather and his extended family. His parents accepted the older two children as grandchildren from the beginning as well. As the older children began school, the oldest child, who had been using his birth surname, came home from school one day and said to his stepfather, "Daddy, I'm tired of having to write a different name. I want to be a Smith!"

At the time of this writing, the couple is in the final stages in the legal process for the husband to fully adopting the oldest two children, and they will soon become Smiths.

This is a wonderful redemptive story of what it is like to feel connected, as well as adopted. It is so important for children in their developing ages to know to whom they belong. These two children in this true story felt loved and accepted and were never treated as being different from the two subsequent children. They felt a sense of belonging. The Smiths are seen as one family with the word *step* removed. They are all Smiths because they belong to each other and have no sense of differentiation.

Knowing that we are connected to someone or something helps satisfy our longings to belong and to feel significant. "People experience the life-changing force of healing relationships when something powerful comes out of one and touches something good in another" (Crabb 2005, p. 67). Good, healthy relationships bring out the best in others and are not self-serving. When bringing out the best in another occurs, the sense of belonging is experienced.

On the other hand, fear can hinder our need for connection. We all make countless attempts to connect whether we realize it or not. Yet many of us self-sabotage such attempts by reacting out of fear.

There are two main ways that fear sabotages connecting. One is by aborting one's attempt to connect, which appears as doubting, ignoring, ridiculing or being angry at the person with whom one is trying to connect soon after or during the attempt to connect. Often, people repel others who are trying to connect with them even in the midst of a relationship building stage, in an attempt to avoid being hurt at that point or in the future. People who suffer from Borderline Personality Disorder (BPD) due to their having been abandoned or abused, try to keep others at a distance through anger and ridicule despite their desperate longing to connect. One of the better books on BPD has a title that perfectly describes the condition—*I Hate You, Don't Leave Me* by Dr. Jerold Kreisman and Hal Strauss.

The second is simply avoiding to connect altogether by isolating one's self from others and retreating from another's attempt to connect with us. Generally speaking, the fear is usually a fear of rejection, of being hurt, or of having such low self-esteem that the feeling and belief are that no one would ever want to be connected with us in the first place. Common symptoms of depression such as dysfunctional eating and sleeping habits, low motivation, and negative moods can accompany the fear as can symptoms of anxiety.

Dr. Susan Johnson (2016) suggested a few principles about connection and identified how our core longings are interconnected and not in a hierarchy as I mentioned in chapter 1. As one of our core longings, the sense of belonging is essential in helping us feel safe and secure and identifying who we are, how we're loved, and where we may be going.

The first principle of attachment is that we all have a built-in longing for connection with someone who will respond to us and keep us safe (Johnson 2016). Feeling safe especially in relationships is a by-product of feeling connected.

> This longing is wired in and designed to keep us close to those we can depend on. We are born helpless and stay that way for longer than any other animal on this planet; this need for connection shapes our nervous system and the mass of neurons we call our brain. We see this longing

when children reach for their mothers, in the loving touch
between longtime partners, and in the fellowship of faith
communities as they unite together in praise and worship.
(Johnson 2016, p. 251)

Knowing we can count on significant people in our lives is
essential for security and well-being. This innate desire is a reflection
of the fact that God created us to be in relationship with Him and
others. To be connected is more than an abstract knowledge of
connection—it is a feeling and experience of belonging.

The second principle of attachment science speaks to the result
of the longing to feel connected—namely, providing a safe haven of
peace, comfort, and consolation (Johnson 2016). The Christian faith
in particular fulfills this desire. The scriptures are full of references
to the importance of being connected to God. More important, God
knew so well how He created us with the need for belonging that He
came to us through Jesus to make it clear that connection to Him
was essential not just for eternal life but for a fulfilled and secure life
on earth.

Even before Jesus came to earth, God showed up in person several
times in the Old Testament. God's presence was always evident to
Adam and Eve as Genesis 3:8 describes: "And they heard the sound
of the Lord God walking in the garden in the cool of the day." The
actual Hebrew word for "cool" means "breeze" and it describes how
Adam and Eve felt God's presence. Connection is not always based
on how much time we spend with others or what we do with them.
It is always based on the quality of their presence (Schafler 2017).

The third principle of attachment theory is that loving,
secure connections make us stronger (Johnson 2016). This may
seem opposite of what we often feel as it relates to the conflict

between teenagers and their parents. Men in our current era, who seem to be weaker and more passive than in past generations, may be so because of less-meaningful connections with others and because of a greater tendency to isolate themselves. Thoreau wrote, "The mass of men lead lives of quiet desperation. What is called resignation is confirmed desperation. A stereotyped but unconscious despair is concealed even under what are called the games and amusements of mankind" (Thoreau 2017, p. 4). In these days when technology, sports, and twenty-four hour, seven days a week television programing, replaces social interaction, it doesn't take much to prove the truth of that statement. Our penchant for emailing, texting, and Facebook messaging robs us of precious human contact. Moreover, when we face trouble in life, we naturally tend to pull away from the very people who want to love us and provide support and comfort.

Isolation breeds several destructive habits including:

- Focusing on negative circumstances instead of seeking positive solutions
- Pulling away from natural support systems and processing negative thoughts and emotions by ourselves.

Instead of isolation, troubled individuals should:

- Surround themselves with loving, supportive friends and family who will love, listen to, and encourage them.
- Find fun, safe, enjoyable activities to occupy their minds and time.
- Reconnect with God. Rekindling a personal relationship with the Creator is essential to everyone's health and well-being.

Isolation is an easy trap to fall into but a hard one to escape unless we realize our error and seeks competent, professional help to assist us in our recovery.

The fourth principle is that since we are designed for relationship and belonging, a lack of connection or losing connection hurts profoundly (Johnson 2016). When we discuss core longings and the need to have them fulfilled, it really boils down to two experiences—rejection or acceptance. We all try to avoid rejection and sometimes at all costs. On the other hand, we all crave acceptance and sometimes at all costs as well. "The pain of rejection registers in the same part of the brain and coded in the same way as physical pain." (Johnson 2016, p. 257)

Codependency

As I mentioned in chapter 1, the idea of fitting in is not the same as belonging. Fitting in is when people desire to be a part of a group or to have a personal relationship with another but the group or individual dictates to those seeking relationship whom they are supposed to be, how they are to act, and what defines them. Those seeking to fit in lose themselves in the group or in someone else and become defined by others. They care for the others in the group and relationships at the expense of caring for themselves. This is the essence of codependency—allowing ourselves to be defined by another to the point that we give up our power to be true to ourselves. Everyone in such a relationship is required to essentially be the same one to another and have the same mind-set or they would not fit in. When it comes to one's identity, "a community must never take precedence over individuals" (Vanier 2003, p. 21).

Codependents often report that they don't know who they are (Mellody 2003). Subby defines codependency this way:

An emotional, psychological, and behavioral condition that
develops as a result of an individual's prolonged exposure
to, and practice of, a set of rules—rules which prevent the
open expression of feelings as well as the direct discussion
of personal and interpersonal problems. (Subby 1984, p. 26)

As this form of dependence on the group develops, it becomes
difficult to break away from it. Street gangs, secret societies, fraternal
organizations, and even religious organizations and churches, are
often more about fitting in than a sense of belonging. Here are some
characteristics of codependency:

- Rescuing or enabling another person
- Low self-worth
- Repression of emotions
- Obsessions about problems or people
- Excessive worry
- A desire and tendency to control people and all situations
- Denying and ignoring problems
- Dependency on others for happiness and identity
- Poor communication including blaming, coercing, and avoidance of important issues
- Weak or nonexistent boundaries
- Lack of trust including of self
- Depression, anxiety, or anger problems—seeming always close to exploding (Beattie 1992)

In most relationships, we live by expectations and requirements.
When we accept a job offer, for example, we know we will have to
accept certain conditions. We choose to comply to gain the benefit

of a job and an income. We often choose activities the same way. We know or learn the rules of a game or the guidelines of membership that come with the specific activity. Even if we are not fully aware of the parameters, we are signing up to become educated and trained about them. Requirements and expectations are a part of the choices we make.

On the other hand, expectations and requirements can be dictated to us in many situations. They are often forced upon us, and we can incorrectly feel that they are self-determined. However, that can be part of the deception, namely, that some expectations and requirements placed on us by others, are our own by which we are to live. When such expectations and requirements are not a part of what we truly want, we feel we must adhere to them to fit in.

When the need to be accepted *no matter what* drives a person to live up to others' expectations, the individual tends to compromise internal integrity and self-identity to avoid rejection. When self-worth is driven by the desire to *fit in*, the "real me" will not truly feel a sense of belonging. A friend and colleague once posted this:

> The drive to fit in is unhealthy because it distorts the genuine human need to belong. It will force you to assume an outward expression that's similar to those whose acceptance and approval you seek while compromising who you truly are. In order to stand out from the crowd, it's vital that your outer expression be a demonstration of inner reality where there has been renewed development of your true-to-God identity. (Chironna 2015)

When the authentic person is accepted, a true sense of belonging is experienced. But when we simply try to fit in, we often experience anxiety because we may never really know if we are successful in being accepted in the group. The liberating power of the gospel in the sacrificial death and resurrection of Jesus saves us to be who we were created to be with our individual personality, gifts, and talents and at the same time, function in a community with a true sense of belonging.

Codependents struggle with self-esteem. Many codependents don't merely dislike themselves; they actually hate themselves (Beattie 1992). Self-esteem is usually linked to external things such as how people look, how much money they make, who they know, what kind of cars they drive, what neighborhoods they live in, what jobs they have, their degrees, and how powerful, important, or attractive their spouses are (Mellody 2003).

Essentially, codependent people are all about human doing and not being secure in themselves as human beings. Mellody (2003) observed, "The problem is that the source of other-esteem is outside the self and thus vulnerable to changes beyond one's control. One can lose this exterior source of esteem at any time, so other-esteem is fragile and undependable" (p. 9).

Codependency develops especially in an environment in which dysfunction and abuse exist. Those who try to fit in take on the impossible role of being sure they are perfect in all that they do or by pleasing those around them. The false belief is that by pleasing certain others, they can "calm the outsized, uncontrollable, and irrational feelings that tyrannize them" (Mellody 2003, p. xiv). Or that they may prevent ever having to be rejected, betrayed, or abandoned. "They live in the delusion that the bad feelings (that they sometimes find almost overwhelming) can be quelled if they can just, 'do it better' or win the approval of certain people in their lives" (Mellody 2003, p. xiv).

Essentially, codependents often seek to control their environments to assure their safety and predictability due to the chaos they experienced as victims of abuse. As a result, their attempts to control their environments coupled with their desire to belong, place them in relationships that lack substance and true intimacy and are unsatisfying. What we experience as a result is codependence and anxiety because we essentially never really know if we fulfilled all that was required of us, causing us to fear that we don't fit in.

Codependents often struggle with distinguishing between boundaries and walls. Though we all have an innate desire to belong, we should employ some helpful and wise aspects to situate ourselves in good relationships. While I have discussed aspects of attachment, boundaries allow for some level of detachment, which can be healthy in relationships. "Detachment does not mean we don't care. It means we learn to love, care, and be involved without going crazy" (Beattie 1992, p. 63). These positive and wisdom-driven considerations are considered boundaries. Mellody (2003) suggested that boundaries have three purposes: "To keep people from coming into our space and abusing us; to keep us from going into others' space and abusing them; and to give each of us a way to embody our sense of who we are" (p. 11).

Boundaries are designed to protect, but walls are designed to isolate. Boundaries allow people to enter into good, healthy, and positive relationships thereby satisfying the sense of belonging we all crave. On the other hand, walls keep people out thereby causing the person who builds personal walls to feel separated and unable to connect.

Detachment is a part of wall also, but the level and reason for the detachment hinder the ability to form healthy relationships and prevent satisfying our sense of belonging. Walls are built for two main reasons: anger and fear. Anger walls give off the message that if you get too close, I will not be happy, I am impatient, and I will explode if things don't go my way or if people don't meet my expectations. The result is that other people become afraid to approach or engage in a relationship for fear of triggering the anger. On the other hand, "People who use a wall of fear retreat from others to keep safe" (Mellody 2003, p. 16). These people refrain from parties, after-work gatherings, and other events. Walls of fear are used based on anxiety—the feeling of insecurity in themselves and in relationships in general. Yet these individuals still yearn for a sense of belonging and connecting with others.

Anxiety prevents us from experiencing peace and true acceptance. I define anxiety as the fear that love, abundance, and competence are in limited supply. In other words, it is a matter of feeling whether we are *loved* enough, *have* enough, or *are* enough. I have spent time with many who report they did not feel they were good enough or did not measure up. Such feelings come from feelings of abandonment (those to whom we were supposed to have belonged are gone), expectations, and requirements of others thereby rendering us unsure if we had ever met them. The common but vague penetrating affliction of low self-worth, where we don't feel good about ourselves or we don't like ourselves, contributes to the concern (Beattie 1992). People can exert so much emotional, mental, and even physical energy too meet others' expectations that they break down. In such cases, they are forever on the move to meet those expectations to gain acceptance, but they do not know if they are successful.

In the 1981 movie *Chariots of Fire*, Harold Abrahams, the 1924 world-class sprinter and eventual Olympic gold medal winner in the 100-meter dash in Paris, made a poignant declaration about his life. He came from a well-to-do Jewish family and attended Cambridge University but felt he had to live up to so many others' expectations.

Discrimination against Jews was common, and he no doubt experienced that in his life. Most Jews felt ridiculed, ostracized, and rejected, and that prevented them from feeling a part of a community outside their own.

His dreams of fame and of proving to his anti-Semitic fellow students and the world that Jews were in no respect inferior ruled his life. Yet when he observed the peace and contentment in one of his classmates and track teammates, Aubrey Montague, he became aware of his own anxiety and sense of trying to fit in. He said to Montague, "That's your secret; contentment. I am twenty-four, and I've never know it. I'm forever in pursuit, and I don't even know what it is I'm chasing." That is what people experience when they are chasing the desire to belong and find out who they are but are attempting to do so in their own power.

In contrast, true belonging is when you are accepted into a group or relationship as yourself. Those who know their strengths and weaknesses develop an authentic understanding of their identities. How you are defined and what you do is acknowledged, accepted, and even valued with no attempts to redefine you. You are valued for who you are and what you contribute to the group by just being you. When you are comfortable in your own skin and at ease in your environment, the real you has no need to fit in—it already does because you belong.

The drive to fit in is unhealthy because it distorts the genuine human need to belong. The deception is that it feels like the same thing. It will force you to assume an outward expression similar to those whose acceptance and approval you seek while compromising who you truly are. In order to stand out from the crowd, your outer expression must be a demonstration of an inner reality where there has been a renewed development of your true-to-God identity.

If we feel accepted based on others' assessments and expectations, we are fitting in. And we are never able to feel secure in our standing in any group because our standing is based on others' assessments of who we are. If we are accepted as who we are based on our true feelings and identity, we experience belonging.

Maya Angelou (1928—2014), an American author, poet, and civil rights activist, suggested there were four questions we unconsciously asking ourselves and each other constantly:

- Do you see me?
- Do you care that I'm here?
- Am I enough for you, or do you need me to be better in some way?
- Can I tell that I'm special to you by the way that you look at me? (Schafler 2017).

People who don't get answers to these questions or worse—receive a no—feel increasingly disconnected from any sense of community (Schafler 2017). Whether it's your children, colleagues, spouse, or anyone in your community, when someone feels generally appreciated, it is because of the positive answers to all four of the above questions. We do not just want someone to simply look at us—we all want to be seen.

One reason people love dogs so much is that dogs answer all four of these questions with an emphatic, yes. Those critters are always in the present moment, and their owners feel connected to them and unconditionally loved by them. It is not just a meaningless cliché that a dog is man's best friend. People and men in particular love their dogs because of the unconditional love and acceptance dogs convey. Many military combat trauma veterans for example love their dogs because they provide them predictable acceptance and peace, things that were diminished as a result of trauma. A sense of calming and attachment to a living creature that provides unconditional love, devotion, safety, and acceptance is therapeutic. No matter what we do, we will feel connected to our pooches and they will feel excitedly connected to us.

In a romantic context, when the above questions go unanswered, the person unconsciously asking them typically becomes increasingly distant, grows restless in the relationship, and often starts looking for excitement, distractions. When someone else answers these questions for them, they feel more alive (Schafler 2017). Often, what looks to be love is in reality rescuing and enabling. Codependents rescue and enable because they give the false appearance of caring for someone, but both are destructive forms of helping (Beattie 1992). Because of the drive to belong to someone, codependents will rescue and enable others who are involved in destructive behaviors and addictions and who simply seem to be victims of misunderstandings. Pity, extreme responsibility, and saintliness are some of the feelings that are mistaken for love.

If mistaken for love, rescuing and enabling will lead people to do things they do not want to do. Such a behavior is also the basis of sin, which simply means "missing the mark." When a codependent misses the mark of love, rescuing and enabling will look like this:

- doing something we really don't want to do
- saying yes when we mean no
- doing something for someone although that person is capable of and should be doing it for himself or herself
- meeting people's needs without being asked and before we've agreed to do so

- doing more than a fair share of work after our help is requested
- consistently giving more than we receive in a particular situation
- fixing people's feelings
- doing people's thinking for them
- speaking for another person
- suffering people's consequences for them
- solving people's problems for them
- putting more interest and activity into a joint effort than the other person does
- not asking for what we want, need, and desire (Beattie 1992, 85)

Some of these concepts coincide with the Word of God. For example, in regard to giving, the Bible makes it clear that when we give, we are to do so with freedom and with purpose (2 Cor. 9:7) understanding that whoever gives sparingly will reap sparingly and whoever gives generously will reap generously (2 Cor. 9:6). Yet 2 Corinthians 8:12 says, "For if the readiness is present, it is acceptable according to what a person has, not according to what he does not have." This verse clearly encourages us that giving within our means is acceptable.

Admittedly, Jesus's teachings may seem to go against these concepts such as encouraging us to go the extra mile for someone (Matt. 5:41). In many cases, God's Word does indeed conflict with contemporary or worldly wisdom. For example, James 4:4 states, "You adulteresses, do you not know that friendship with the world is hostility toward God? Therefore whoever wishes to be a friend of the world makes himself an enemy of God." Also, Romans 12:2 declares, "And do not be conformed to this world, but be transformed by the renewing of your mind, so that you may prove what the will of God is, that which is good and acceptable and perfect."

On the other hand, what may seem to be in conflict may simply be a misunderstanding of the teachings of scripture. To turn the other cheek does not imply pacifism or putting ourselves or others in mortal danger. Turning the other cheek refers to personal retaliation, not criminal offenses or acts of military aggression. It refers to our tendency toward vengeance and does not negate the wisdom of self-protection. Clearly, Jesus did not mean to negate all God's laws and injunctions protecting us against violent crime or invading armies. Rather, Jesus was speaking here of the principle of not retaliating for affronts against our dignity as well as lawsuits to gain personal assets (v. 40), infringements on liberty (v. 41), and violations of property rights (v. 42). He was calling for a full surrender of all personal rights. Turning the other cheek means not to return insult for insult in retaliation, which is what most people expect and how worldly people act.

Therefore, the scriptures speak of the spirit of giving and righteous behaviors as being for another person's good. The spirit of codependency on the other hand is giving so we would feel good or be accepted by others. The contrast in motivation is critically important to understand.

The next chapter discusses community and how a sense of belonging and connectedness can develop into a community that provides mutual support and encouragement.

CHAPTER 5

Community

And I will say ... "You are my people"; and he shall say,
"Thou are my God."

—Hosea 2:23 (KJV)

But if we walk in the light as He Himself is in the light,
we have fellowship with one another.

—1 John 1:7

A sense of belonging develops through the feeling of connectedness, which always occurs in the context of community. People cannot feel they belong unless they are part of a community of some kind. People cannot experience community without feeling they belong. As a result, to be a part of a community is feeling we belong somewhere and to someone.

The purpose of belonging to a community is not just for the growth of the community at the expense of the individual; belonging is for becoming (Vanier 2003). In our society and in many other cultures, we are becoming increasingly more individualistic. The problem that results from this trend is that personal character development becomes retarded and skewed. A sense of belonging is meant to help us feel good when we are connected and to bring out the best in one another. Crabb observed,

> Character that enables love develops best when hidden issues of the heart (primarily deep longings and self-protective relational strategies) are directly addressed, and the ideal soil for character growth is rich community. Only in personal interaction can hidden issues of the heart be substantially surfaced and resolved. (Crabb 2013, p. 229)

Because of the hard work that building relationships and community requires, more and more individuals are remaining solitary because they perceive that to be easier. The result, however, is the inability to know how to get along, recover from disappointments, feel support from caring others, and every human being's biggest fear—rejection.

One of the often overlooked aspects of marriage is the ability of spouses to bring out the best in each other. Even in the midst of conflict and disappointment, the mission of both spouses can be completed, and it is an essential benefit of character growth. It also is the mission of any healthy community. I can attest to at least two factors of my character development. First, marriage changed me from a self-oriented twenty-four-year-old into a husband who increasingly became more aware of how to love his wife. Second, having our five children (a growing community impact without a doubt) also made me grow up in a hurry though I went kicking and screaming into certain areas of dying to self before emerging as a changed individual.

Community, the foundational family unit, will indeed make or break us, and character development benefits the family and the community at large. The common cliché about people getting married is they are settling down, but there is much scientific and relational truth to that. The promise of permanency makes marriage more of a beneficial relationship than simply living together. The greater perceived security has an effect on both parties. A sense of belonging one to another has positive effects on a couple's financial picture. Married men are more successful in work; they are promoted more often and receive higher performance appraisals. They also miss work or arrive late less often (Waite and Gallagher 2001). White married women without children earn 4 percent more, and black married women earn 10 percent more than their single peers (Waite and Gallagher 2001).

Married people live longer as well. Single men have mortality rates that are 250 percent higher than those of married men. Single women have mortality rates 50 percent higher than those of married women (Waite and Gallagher 2001). Having a spouse can decrease your risk of dying from cancer as much as knocking ten years off your life. Single people spend longer in the hospital and have a greater risk of dying after surgery (Waite and Gallagher 2001). Married women are 30 percent more likely to rate their health as excellent or very good compared to single women, and they are 40 percent less likely to rate their health as only fair or poor compared to single women. Based on life expectancies, nine of ten married men and women alive at age forty-eight are alive at sixty-five, while only six of ten single men and eight of ten single women make it to sixty-five (Waite and Gallagher 2001).

In terms of mental health, married men are half as likely to commit suicide as single men are and a third as likely as divorced men are. Widowed men under age forty-five are nine times more likely to commit suicide than are married men. Married people report lower levels of depression and distress, and 40 percent say they are very happy with their lives compared to about 25 percent in single people. Married people were half as likely to say they were unhappy with their lives (Waite and Gallagher 2001). Single men drink twice as much as married men do, and one out of four say their drinking causes problems, while only one of seven married men says the same (Waite and Gallagher 2001).

Greater safety studies assessing risk for violence are sometimes used to indicate that women by being married are at risk for violence. Waite and Gallagher (2001) argue that many studies treat husbands, boyfriends, paramours, and ex-partners all the same. As a result, "wife battering" should be separated from domestic abuse, and wife battering should refer only to abuse in the context of a marriage. Studies also do not distinguish between domestic violence and abuse.

When it comes to violence, wives are five times less likely than single or divorced women to be victims of crime, and husbands are four times less likely to be victims of crime than are single or divorced men (Waite and Gallagher 2001). Thus, Waite and Gallagher (2001) conclude that less than 2 percent of wives and less than 1 percent of husbands are abused by the common definition each year, and they argue that married partners look out for each other's safety and warn each other about risks. They are also less likely to be violent with each other as they have a greater investment in the relationship. They are more integrated into a network of friends and family and are not as isolated as a result. The strength of community and the sense of belonging make a difference.

If the Bible is our guide, we would do well to understand how often the concept of community is taught. The Bible encourages healthy community by the verses that address "one another." There are a hundred verses in the New Testament alone that deal with the "one another" dynamic. Jesus, Peter, John, Paul, and James all taught the importance of how we treat one another. The essence of community rests on the way we treat one another. For example, we are commanded to stimulate one another to love and good deeds (Heb. 10:24). Colossians 3:13 directs us to bear with and forgive one another as Christ does us. Also, we are to clothe ourselves with humility toward one another (1 Peter 5:5).

One of the more complete encouragements about community life is in 1 Thessalonians 5:11–15.

> Therefore encourage one another, and build up one another, just as you also are doing. But we request of you, brethren, that appreciate those who diligently labor among you, and have charge over you in the Lord and give you instruction, and that you esteem them very highly in love because of their work. Live in peace with one another. And we urge you, brethren, admonish the unruly, encourage the fainthearted, help the weak, be patient with all men. See that no one repays another with evil for evil, but always seek after that which is good for one another and for all men.

In this verse addressing us—the church, the community of believers and followers of Christ—we are commanded to honor those in authority as well as those who labor among us. In a community, everyone has an important role, and mutual respect is essential. Notice how it is as important to "admonish the unruly" as it is to "help the weak." A healthy community is dependent upon both aspects of discipline and care, order and compassion, law and grace. The one without the other leads to chaos, lawlessness, self-centeredness, and violence. No community can withstand either extreme.

There are many forms of community that offer a sense of belonging. Essentially, community begins with the family. Vanier pointed out:

> Many of its points apply equally to family life. The two essential elements of life in community are also part of life in a family: inter-personal relationship, a sense of belonging and an orientation of life to a common goal and common witness. (Vanier 2003, p. 10)

God began culture and community with a wedding of a man and a woman. Since the married couple is the essence and foundation of any family community, many studies have shown that married couples are generally healthier and live longer than divorced or single people do. The sense of connectedness and belonging provides great benefits to married people. Research consistently finds married men and women are:

- more likely to live longer,
- more likely to be physically healthier,
- more likely to be mentally healthier,
- more likely to be happier,
- more likely to recover from illness quicker and more successfully, and
- more likely to take better care of themselves and avoid risky behavior. (Waite and Gallagher 2000; Wilson and Oswald 2005)

Wilson and Oswald (2005) found that the health benefits are so significant that one sociologist described them as being as "large as the benefit from giving up smoking" (p. 16).

For men and women, the sense of belonging also provides mental and emotional stability. Belonging for men brings a sense of acceptance, connectedness, competence, accomplishment, and respect. Belonging for women brings a sense of acceptance, connectedness, security, love, and value.

In a family, there is extended family from the husband's and wife's sides. Several families living as neighbors can develop into a neighborhood. The neighborhood develops in a town. As a small town grows, a city may develop. And on this goes up to and including a nation and then a culture. The awareness of our connectedness, our community, is an important aspect of feeling we belong.

Besides the family and the extensions of families are other communities that contribute to the individual's longing to belong. One common community is a local church. The diverse nature of a church along with the commonality of belief in God can be an important way of feeling connected even for others not like ourselves in appearance. The unity God enjoys as a triune God expressed in the Father, Son, and Holy Spirit is an essential part of His kingdom. God's kingdom experience begins with relationship with Him through Jesus and empowered by His Holy Spirit. The personal experience is followed by becoming a part of a community of believers. Paul described the sense of belonging in a church context this way:

> And the eye cannot say to the hand, "I have no need of you"; or again the head to the feet, "I have no need of you." On the contrary, it is much truer that the members of the body which seem to be weaker are necessary; and

those members of the body which we deem less honorable, on these we bestow more abundant honor, and our less presentable members become much more presentable, whereas our more presentable members have no need of it. But God has so composed the body, giving more abundant honor to that member which lacked, so that there may be no division in the body, but that the members may have the same care for one another. And if one member suffers, all the members suffer with it; if one member is honored, all the members rejoice with it. (1 Cor. 12:21–26)

A true sense of belonging recognizes the gifts and contributions that all members provide without competition because all are secure in their individuality as well as their positions in the group. There is also a sense of encouragement to all without a sense of one person being more valuable than another. There is support, encouragement, identity, mutual participation, and purpose when a person is a part of a distinct community like the church.

Unfortunately, as the family has become broken and even redefined, so also have churches experienced increasing brokenness as well. Vanier wrote,

For many centuries, communities were linked to institutional churches, but today in many places the influence of these churches is waning. Community is the place of meeting with God … It is the place of belonging; it is the place of growth in love. Individualism and materialism lead to rivalry, competition and the rejection of the weak. (Vanier 2003, p. 8)

While there are many great things about our culture in the United States, one of the detriments is the overemphasis on individualism. Individualism brings a sense of self-centeredness and a focus on individual rights that often undermine the attempt to create community. James wrote,

> For where jealousy and selfish ambition exist, there is disorder and every evil thing. But the wisdom from above is first pure, then peaceable, gentle, reasonable, full of mercy and good fruits, unwavering, without hypocrisy. And the seed whose fruit is righteousness is sown in peace by those who make peace. (James 3:16-18)

Stine observed, "True community is fostered in an environment where everyone is encouraged to be whom God made them to be— when the God-given differences that make each person unique are celebrated and welcomed" (Stine 2017, p. 236).

Sports teams as well as school bands, drama clubs, and graduating classes can all provide a similar sense of belonging, support, camaraderie, and identity. Those on a team are encouraged to work together for a common goal. While there may be individual standouts on a team, he or she could not be one without other teammates playing their parts. Sports such as track and field, cross-country, swimming, diving, tennis, and golf are more individualistic and may provide a lesser sense of community, but being on such a team still fosters a sense of belonging in its members.

Being in the military is another community that fosters a tremendous sense of belonging. The military community has its own language and customs, and only those in the community understand these nuances. Training in the military is focused on leaving no one behind, togetherness as it relates to the mission at hand, and a shared sense of loss when a comrade goes down. Soldiers and vets who suffer post-traumatic stress disorder (PTSD) often want to isolate themselves, but treatment for PTSD includes helping them reintegrate and reengage with their primary support groups, usually their families. "Families can help the veteran avoid withdrawal from others. Families can provide companionship and a sense of belonging, which can help counter feelings of separateness and difference from other people" (Lawhorne and Philpott 2010, p. 149).

Churches can also undergird the sense of support and belonging that can be especially critical when warriors come home wounded or grieving the loss of comrades, mentally affected by PTSD, and morally confused as to what they experienced in combat situations. One veteran wrote about these challenges:

> Veterans need a sense of belonging. In the military we call that sense of belonging, unit cohesion. Unit cohesion is something that is difficult to reproduce in the civilian world. The closest likeness might be taking part in a sports team, but like most, I haven't been part of a sports team since I was in high school. However, I do have a place that provides me with a sense of belonging—my church. The church has supported my military career every step of the way in tangible ways … care packages galore, letters, emails. They even collected soccer balls so I could give them away to Iraqi children. My church has given me an excellent sense of support and belonging. The men of my small group Bible study took care of incidentals that came up with my family while I was deployed. They even replaced my back porch to surprise me when I returned home! I have

recently discovered that one of the best things my church does is provide me with a sense of belonging, especially the guys in my small group Bible study. We've been meeting for over nine years and we are close friends. As it turns out, having close friends and a solid sense of belonging is critical for healthy transitions from war to peace, from military to civilian. I credit Christ and His church for meeting the deep needs of my soul—belonging and mission. In the Church, we call that sense of belonging—that unit cohesion, Christian community. *Celebrate Recovery* does that better than anything else we've got going at my church. The Open Share groups and the Step Studies are the closest models we have for producing unit cohesion in civilian life. *Celebrate Recovery* is perfectly poised to step into the veteran's community and offer real solutions to the transitional issues they are facing. It's the perfect opportunity for us to invite them into the *Celebrate Recovery* family for belonging. It's the perfect opportunity to offer them the Gospel of Jesus Christ and to join the worldwide mission that is the Great Commission. (Pitts 2016)

The sense of family is the essence of the sense of community. Without family, the longing for belonging seeks fulfillment elsewhere. "The deepest yearning in a child is to be in communion with its mother and father." (Vanier 2003, p. 13)

The Table

In most cultures around the world, community and a sense of belonging revolves around family or tribal meals. Sitting with others for a meal encourages fellowship, unity, and care. To satisfy one of life's essential needs—nourishment—with others is an obvious way to demonstrate a communal sense of care. Others invited to a meal are honored by that, enjoy fellowship and care, and feel a part of the unity in the community. An Eastern proverb states, "The guest while in the house is its lord." Lot had this posture as we read in Genesis 19:2: "Behold now, my lords, turn in, I pray you, into your servant's house."

In the Far East, sharing meal is a special act of hospitality that means far more that it means in the Western world (Wight 1953). It is a sign of acceptance into the hosts' community, of peacemaking, and of desire for meaningful fellowship. That is why the Last Supper was more than just a meal in the upper room (Luke 22:1–23). Jesus was establishing a new covenant (v. 20) and inviting them into His community, the kingdom of God. The Middle Eastern mind-set understood that Jesus was inviting the disciples into the kingdom He was trying to establish.

The parable that Jesus taught of the marriage supper in Matthew 22:1–14 is another example of a sense of belonging in a community. The wedding banquet was one of the most joyous occasions in Jewish life and could last for a week. In His parable, Jesus compared heaven to a wedding banquet a king had prepared for his son. Many people had been invited, but when the time for the banquet came and the table was set, those invited refused to come (vv. 4–5). In fact, the king's servants who brought the joyful message were mistreated and even killed (v. 6). Enraged at the response of those who had been invited, the king sent his army to avenge the deaths of his servants (v. 7). He then sent invitations to anyone his servants could find with the result that the wedding hall was filed (vv. 8–10).

The parable conveyed how God sent His Son into the world, and the very people who should have celebrated His coming rejected Him and brought judgment upon themselves. As a result, the community of the kingdom of heaven was opened to those who would set aside their righteousness and by faith accept the righteousness God provides in Christ. Those who spurn the gift of salvation by their refusal to come to the banquet will not enjoy the benefits of the community of God. Though they desire to belong, those who refuse the invitation will not experience belonging.

Abraham Rihbany (1869–1944), an American theologian and historian who was born in Lebanon, added to the understanding of the importance of meals in the cultural context. In his book *The Syrian Christ*, he explained the cultural background of some situations and modes of expression found in the Gospels. One example related to the importance of sharing a meal:

> An Oriental considers as sacred the expression, "bread and salt." When it is said, "There is bread and salt between us" it is the same as saying, "We are bound together by a solemn covenant." A foe will not "taste the salt" of his adversary unless he is ready to be reconciled to him. (Rihbany 1916, p. 191)

This depicts the need to be reconciled with an individual in order to break bread and restore relationship in the community. The sense of belonging may be predicated on how the two parties desire to seek reconciliation and become friends again.

However, "among oriental people, when a covenant of friendship has been once broken, it may be renewed by those involved once again by eating together" (Wight 1953, p. 78). When Jacob and Laban strained their relationship, they restored it by eating together; by doing so, they made a covenant (Gen. 31:53–54). After Jesus's resurrection, when the disciples scattered and Peter even betrayed Him, Jesus ate with them again at least three times to restore the relationship and the covenant (Luke 24:30, 41–43; John 21:12–13).

One of the many benefits of sharing a meal in Eastern cultures is that hosts will defend their guests from all possible enemies and harm during the time of their relationship (Wight 1953). This is depicted in the popular Psalm 23: "Thou dost prepare a table before me in the presence of my enemies" (v. 5). The concept is clear: Jesus made a meal for us, the Sacrament of Communion, to establish a new covenant, restore a relationship with us, provide protection from our enemies especially Satan and eternal death, and allow us to enjoy an honored place in His community. All of these aspects ultimately satisfy the sense of belonging all people desire.

In our culture, the importance of having meals together as a family has truly diminished. While the American culture never held the level of importance of sharing a meal that was understood in Eastern cultures, we nevertheless appreciated and benefitted from meals together. Throughout American history, having meals together was indicative of celebration, fellowship, acceptance, and a feeling of belonging. During the early and mid-twentieth century, when two-parent nuclear families were the norm in middle-class America, family dinners at home were a common evening ritual. When Dad came home after a hard day's work, Mom would have dinner waiting for him. Kids might have after-school activities but were usually required to be home in time for dinner (Kiefer 2004). Children often knew that mealtime was a time to discuss the day's events and feel accepted and encouraged despite their discouragements. As a result, the need to look elsewhere for a sense of community and belonging was foreign to most families.

Today, the average family does not enjoy meals together as in the past due to many factors such as the splintered or broken nuclear family structure, our impossible busy lifestyles, the abuse and pain that has increasingly become the family experience, and the increased mobility of family members who are no longer living close to one another to name just a few.

According to the Bureau of Labor Statistics, 78 percent of women with children between ages six and seventeen work outside the home. Figures from the 2000 census show that 31 percent of households with children are single-parent families, and that is up from 13 percent in 1970. Kids take part in more after-school activities than ever, and many parents have to go straight from work to soccer practice, piano lessons, or car pools. There simply isn't much time for cooking, and eating is often done on the run.

A Gallup poll (December 11–14, 2003) of 331 American adults aged eighteen or older with children under age eighteen confirmed that having dinner together in the evening was difficult for today's families. Slightly more than a quarter of adults (28%) with children under age of eighteen reported that their families at dinner together at home seven nights a week; that was down from 37 percent in 1997. Almost half (47%) of parents said their families at together between four and six times a week. And 24 percent said they ate together three or fewer nights a week (Kiefer 2017).

According to an August 2003 Gallup Youth Survey, 20 percent of teenagers ages thirteen to seventeen ate fast food either every day or several times a week. Considering the rising prominence of youth obesity as a national health problem, it seems that teens could certainly benefit health-wise from eating more meals at home.

Also, dinnertime might be one of the few opportunities during the day that parents get to talk with their children about what's happening in their lives. All parents want to know what's going on with their children, but a 2003 study by the National Center on Addiction and Substance Abuse at Columbia University suggested that family dinners could have some concrete benefits for teenagers. The study found that teens who had dinner with their families two nights a week or less were twice as likely to take drugs, more likely to be "high stress," more likely to say they were often bored, and less likely to perform well in school than teens who ate with their families five to seven times a week.

Number of Nights Families Eat Together at Home (United States)

How many nights a week out of seven does your family eat dinner together at home?

Asked of U.S. adults with children under age 18

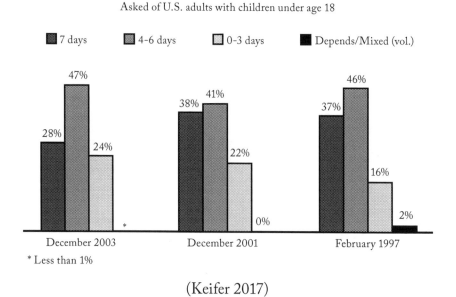

December 2003   December 2001   February 1997
* Less than 1%

(Keifer 2017)

The Book

One other measure of community is an item often overlooked. There is a common cliché that many people use that creates a positive sense in the recipient. When a person states, "You're okay in my book," the connotation is one of acceptance and affirmation. The word picture suggests that we all have a book and that when we are written in it, we are accepted and belong to the holder of the book.

Most families have baby books that list the many developmental milestones of their children—a child's first step, first word, when they were potty trained, and when they could name the primary colors just to name a few. When children are older and can look back through their books, they can derive a sense of accomplishment, how they grew in their families, and belonging because they can see the pride their parents felt throughout their development. Often, such details of their development, especially because it was written, conveys to the child they were wanted and celebrated.

Guest books are often used for important events such as weddings and funerals. The names recorded in these guest books will forever be reminders for the couple getting married or the family who lost a loved one whom others supported and valued. Such books can give a sense of belonging to those who wrote their names in the book as if they were a part of the host family for that event. It also brings a sense of belonging to those who were married that day or who lost a loved one because they can see that others cared enough to be with them during such happy and sad times alike.

High school seniors treasure their yearbooks and ask fellow students and teachers to sign them and make a statement or two. Their yearbooks will forever be emotional reminders of an important community to which they belonged, especially during the important developmental experiences as teenagers. Former students bring their yearbooks to reunions to see how much others have changed and relive memories with them. Yearbooks also provide a memorial of sorts such as when a classmate dies. They always brings a sense of belonging to a community that has affected our formative years.

In today's world, another book—Facebook—provides a growing

sense of a global community and helps fulfill the longing for belonging and connectedness to others. Facebook, founded in Cambridge, Massachusetts, in February 2004 by Mark Zuckerberg and others, has become a social media sensation. As of the third quarter of 2017, Facebook had 2.07 billion monthly active users (Statista 2017). Facebook connects us to old friends and to new friends with whom we may spend many hours exchanging posts or messages. The number of friends even if casual and simply listed brings a sense of belonging when we believe we have 684 "friends." In reality, no one has that many friends, but it nonetheless brings a sense of belonging to having such a large of network of those who we believe may "care" about us.

Christians have a book too, the one in which their names are written if they believe in Jesus. The apostle Paul called it the book of life (Phil. 4:3). The apostle John mentioned this book at least twenty-eight times in the book of Revelation and even called it the Lamb's book of life (Rev. 21:27). This book belongs to the Lamb of God, and He is the only one who can manage it and open it (Rev. 5).

Community provides a sense of belonging for several reasons. It provides a place for caring to take place. It begins with the nuclear family, a place where cooperation can develop and grow. Community provides a place of healing and restoration and it provides a place for forgiveness and mutual trust to develop. It provides an environment for individuals to grow and develop and it is a place of acceptance even when we show weaknesses. Community provides a place of hope.

However, many things affect a sense of belonging and the security that having a true sense of community brings. The next two chapters discuss several of the forces that reduce and even eliminate a true sense of belonging.

CHAPTER 6

When a Sense of Belonging Is Missing—Family

There is neither Jew nor Greek, there is neither slave nor free man, there is neither male nor female; for you are all one in Christ Jesus. And if you belong to Christ, then you are Abraham's offspring, heirs according to promise.

—Galatians 3:28–29

For he Himself has said, "I will never desert you, nor will I ever forsake you."

—Hebrews 13:5

Isaac, a twenty-five-year-old African-American graduate student, came to counseling to discuss his anxiety issues as it related to his relationships and vocational direction. At the time of our first session, he had been married for three years to a wonderful woman and their first baby was on the way.

As he revealed his background and story, he spoke of a disjointed family environment. The second youngest of nine children, he had grown up in the "projects" with multiple fathers and one mother who never married. Isaac expressed a deep deficiency in terms of a sense of family. His mother had abandoned the family when he was sixteen; he and his younger brother were cared for by an older sister in a different community. We I began to meet with Isaac, he had not seen his mother for a long time and never knew a father.

Isaac said that many of his friends had moved away or developed other interests thereby reducing their time with him and he said a mentor of his had passed away suddenly. Whenever Isaac thought of his future, his anxiety would increase to the point that he would retreat to his room not wanting to engage with others. He said that his only sense of belonging was to his wife, but he admitted that he often wondered why she stayed with him. When I asked whom he felt the most connected to, he said only his wife.

As we processed through his background and story, he was able to see how the lack of a sense of belonging contributed to his inability to feel confident about relationships since many people in his life had simply come and gone. He also discovered that since he did not have anyone speak into his life and help provide him with a sense of belonging, identity, and purpose, he was anxious and he never truly felt competent to fulfill certain adult roles and set vocational goals for himself.

Isaac did have a solid faith in Christ, with whom he felt identified. His love for his wife also allowed him to know that the commitment in the marriage was meaningful enough to provide him a sense of belonging to someone who unconditionally loved him.

The desire to feel like we belong somewhere and to someone is so strong that when it is missing, it results in several alternative outcomes and behaviors. Vanier observed:

When a child feels it does not belong to anyone, it suffers terrible loneliness and this is manifested in anguish. Anguish is like an inner agitation which affects the whole body, transforming the digestive and sleep patterns, bringing confusion, destroying all clarity about what to do, and how to act … according to childhood needs that were not fulfilled, some people want belonging at almost any price. They feel so lonely that they are prepared to sacrifice personal consciousness and growth in order to be part of a group. (Vanier 1989, p. 13–14)

Young people experience a breach in their sense of belonging when their parents' divorce for whatever reason. A broken family can be devastating to a youngster. Also, when a parent leaves the family outright, is never a part of the child-developing relationship in the first place, or mistreats family members, such abandonment and abuse can be devastating to a youngster. Death of a parent or an especially close caregiver can have an effect similar to abandonment. This experience is often exacerbated when a caregiver commits suicide. Suicide itself is often driven by a sense that no one cares anymore.

Divorce

In addition to divorce, I will also include the increasing birthrate of single mothers who in most cases will not have the man involved to assist in raising the child or children. Currently, about 44 percent of all births are now to single mothers (CDCP 2017). The Bible teaches that God hates divorce (Mal. 2:16). When we hear that, we often feel God will hate us if we divorce. Unfortunately, many churches suggest such a concept. Divorce is not the "unforgiveable sin"—there is only one of those, and divorce isn't it (see my book *Created for Understanding* for a discussion of the unforgivable sin).

The truth is that God hates divorce because He knows what it is like to experience unfaithful and broken relationships with those He loves, and He can experience grief according to Ephesians 4:30. One just has to read the Old Testament prophets such as Isaiah, Jeremiah, Hosea, and Amos among others to hear of God's lament and anger toward the unfaithfulness of His people.

God hates the often traumatic residual effects divorce has on the people involved especially children. For example, according to a report cited by the *Richmond Times-Dispatch* in 2013, broken homes account for

- 78 percent of incarcerated men,
- 80 percent of rapists,
- 63 percent of youth suicides,
- 71 percent of high school dropouts,
- 75 percent of all drug users,
- 71 percent of teenage pregnancies, and
- 85 percent of behavioral disorders

The loss of the sense of belonging has had a devastating effect on the young people who during their developmental years seek meaningful attachments even if that means destructive behaviors.

On the other hand, divorce may be the best answer for spouses and children in cases of domestic violence, abuse, or other harmful behavior on the part of one or both parents. Whoever abuses a spouse and children needs to be removed from the home through local law enforcement, local departments of family services, or the county sheriff's office.

In helping children cope with divorce, one must first understand the impact that divorce has on children. Author and researcher Dr. Edward Teyber stated, "One out of three children in America today has divorced parents" (Teyber 2001, p. 1). He also said that these children would develop many forms of anxiety about separation and fears of being abandoned. Separation anxiety can lead to many others forms of alarming behavior that can hinder the formation of long-lasting relationships.

Learning to trust others to form relationships is also a problem for children of divorce. These children—innocent victims of divorce—need help and coping methods to help them through this traumatizing experience (Teyber 2001, p. 1).

In most cases, divorce affects children very abruptly and causes irreparable changes in their lives. Conflict affects the family and consequently the child, in the areas of economics, identity, anger, and fear. Children are often placed with one of their parents in a less than ideal situation that is usually lacking in financial and emotional support. Johnson wrote:

> Attachment scholars also talk of how, when a child has a secure connection with a parent, he or she is able to put his or her inner world together into a coherent whole in which everything makes sense, rather than being pulled in many directions by random ideas and reactive emotions. (Johnson 2016, p. 252)

Victimized children question who they are and begin to wonder where they belong. Because many of these questions are left unanswered, the children can often become angry. Changes in their living situations can result in fear and anxiety.

The impact of divorce on children can be revealed in their sadness, worry, loneliness, and struggles with loss of being. The children are sad and do not quite understand why and they commonly begin to worry if their parents' divorce was their fault. They struggle with loneliness because their family life has been altered, and they may even have to move from friends and family. Children do not understand what is happening, and they begin to question who they are and where they really belong. If their parents remarry, do they belong in either family? Children of divorce can be severely overburdened and will face the adverse effects on their mental well-being through adulthood.

Children can face extreme trauma and stress when a parent leaves suddenly and without explanation or warning. That abrupt departure could be one of the last memories children have of the parent who left. The children may ask themselves, *Why did she leave so suddenly?* or *When will he come back?* or *Who else will leave?* Separation anxiety is a result, and that can develop into a long-lasting fear of abandonment in adulthood (Teyber 2001, p. 27).

Children of conflicting, separated, or divorced parents are always frightened by their parents' arguments. Their main fear is that harm will come to one of their parents; even older children who seem disinterested or aloof can be fearful. Children do not like their parents to be at risk. Many times, children will not express their fears but feel very anxious nonetheless. Children are frightened when they see their parents shout at each other or think that their parents are threatened in any way. Most children when asked express a strong hatred of their parents' fighting and say they wish they would never fight because it scares them (Teyber 2001, p. 81).

Sometimes, children feel responsible for parental conflict. Children often blame themselves for their unhappy parents in an egocentric way and often blame themselves for their parents' divorce. Though parents sometimes fight over their children, that is not usually the cause of the divorce, and the children should be reassured that they did not cause the divorce.

All marital conflict and divorce is destructive for children, but it may be especially harmful to boys. Researchers have discovered that the average boy does not cope with divorce as well as the average girl does. Boys are more vulnerable to the adverse effects of parental conflict; they are usually more sensitive and especially more likely to blame themselves for marital conflict and divorce. Boys also question themselves more about their own being and identity (Root 2010).

After a divorce, traditional child-rearing roles are negatively altered. Divorced parents must understand that the most precious gift they can give their children is time with the former spouse so the children can learn to love the one who left. They need to have the trust renewed with the parent as much as possible. Parents need to give children permission to love and grow close to their ex-spouses. It should be a priority to ensure wholeness and stronger mental health to their wounded child (Teyber 2001, p. 1).

For example, divorce between parents with children is very common in Canada. The divorce rate has increased—one in two marriages ends in divorce. Studies in Canada among researchers have found that divorce causes a decrease in mental health and an increase in vulnerability among children (McGuinness, 2006). In some studies, some post-divorce children were found to be resilient to a degree in the way divorce affected them. Some of their noted character traits were "easy temperament," a sense of humor, and good physical health and intelligence. These children seemed to be able to weather the difficulty better than most (Hetherington 2005). But generally, most children respond to divorce with a degree of emotional distress that usually includes anger, sadness, depression, rebellion, and anxiety. Adolescents' responses can include dropping out of school, substance abuse, and delinquent behavior (McGuinness 2006). Research has shown that parental divorce can affect children and adolescents in mentally adverse ways that continue to their adulthood (Strohscheim 2005).

Many researchers of divorce have concluded that divorce has continual effects on children that often persist throughout adulthood. Children of adults who divorce often become adults who live with economic problems, lower earnings, have children out of wedlock, and generally have a lower quality of life. In his book *The Children of Divorce*, Andrew Root wrote, "Pending divorce feels like an impending ontological security issue and the loss of one's being or self" (Root 2010, p. 121). One older person facing the pending divorce of his parents said he feared losing his sense of being, who he was: "It was the fear that now the union that created me was dissolving, I might dissolve with it" (Root 2010, p. 192).

The longing of children to belong is extremely significant to their emotional well-being. They want to be connected to the origins of their emotional well-being. They want to be connected to the origins of their biological being, both mother and father. When divorced parents remarry into another community, fear of loss of being is increased. "Children no longer feel like they belong, often it feels like a loss of being" (Root 2010, p. 192).

Childhood is usually a time when children are sheltered in the refuge of their families. Researchers have found that children from divorced homes have felt significantly less safe physically and emotionally. Usually, parents have the role of protecting their children, but children of divorced parents often feel a sense of aloneness and expect no help from anyone (Steakley 2008).

The following excerpts come from essays of college students who wrote about their experiences as children of divorce. They convey very common feelings young people whose parents have divorced experience. Notice how the sense of broken belongingness also affected their identity, how they saw their lives, and how it affected their sense of purpose. Two of these young people relate how finding faith in God helped them with a restored sense of belonging. One of those students benefitted from joining the marines, which also provides a strong sense of identity, purpose, and belonging. One individual at the time of his writing seemed to still struggle with feeling connected.

> While my childhood wasn't the worst it definitely wasn't easy. My parents divorced when I was eight and almost immediately they both started dating. I was the youngest child and my brother and sister were already out of the house so I was left alone. I started to resent my parents and started to not care about my education or what happened to me. Once in high school, I started dating and my relationships never lasted long. I thought this was normal since my parents were dating different people every few weeks. I almost adopted their behavior. I started realizing that I didn't really fit in with anyone at school because I felt no one was going through what I was going through. After several moves I ended up going to three different high schools. By this time I had taken control of my education since I didn't have much support from my family. It wasn't until I went to college that I realized that I didn't truly know who I was or what I wanted. I met a girl one day who told me that I should join her one day when she went to

church. That day changed my life. I had never been a very religious person but after going with my friend and talking to fellow Christians it made me realize what it would take to make me happy. I can honestly say that when I got God in my life I finally felt that for once I knew who I was and that I belonged (Male, age twenty).

When I was in middle school in eighth grade, my parents divorced. Although it hit me hard, I didn't show any emotions towards any of my friends. I was always one of the kids who was on sports teams and tried to come off as a tougher individual. Even though I shrugged the divorce off, it tore me apart inside. I fought to stay positive and honestly nothing changed for me outside of that. Still to this day it still bothers me, but I believe it made me a stronger individual today. It is a lesson of how something big can hit someone and how someone can respond to it in the most positive way possible. I never let my peers know I was bothered and it is still the same today. I did my best to postpone the (feeling of) disaster and did anything I could to never think about it and continue to live the way I still am today (Male, age nineteen).

I was nine years old when my parents divorced and it was a real challenging time for me. I was basically raised from that point by my grandparents, and I lost what relationship I had with my father. It took me a long time to understand who I was and who I wanted to be. It was after I joined the United States Marine Corps, that the confusion of who I was started to become clear. It was also while in the Marines that I developed a stronger relationship with God that helped define who I was becoming as a man. I struggled finding out who I was and it wasn't until I put all my faith in God that it all came together for me (Male, age twenty-four).

Though most children of divorce become extremely independent, many appreciate others' advice. Children are usually easily guided if they can trust those around them. Adults must make it their priority to provide guidance to the victimized children in our society. Many appreciate someone giving them advice and gently guiding them through life.

In Psalm 10:14, David spoke of God being a father to the fatherless: "But you do not see, for you note mischief and vexation, that you may take it into your hands, to you the helpless commits himself, you have been the helper of the fatherless."

Though there are many children of divorce in our society, they are not hopeless. The impact divorce has had on these victimized children is serious but can be helped by those who want to be like parents to them. There is hope in that many churches have outreach ministries to divorced parents and their children. It is essential that the church understands the dilemma these children face if they are uncared for and unguided. Because of the potential problems children of divorce face if they are not helped, society must assure that the mental well-being of these children be considered and taken care of as part of its responsibility to them. Children are the next generation who will lead and guide other children with many more complex problems.

The impact of divorce is severe among children and adults and must be faced with realistic help to prepare society for mental well-being and love of life. An NBC News report provides some insight as to the effect of babies without both parents. Dr. Natalie Carroll, an

African-American OB/GYN in Houston, Texas, cites that 72 percent of black babies are born to unmarried mothers today according to government statistics. This number is inseparable from the work of Carroll, an obstetrician who has dedicated her forty-year career to helping black women. "The girls don't think they have to get married. I tell them children deserve a mama and a daddy. They really do," Carroll said in the report (Washington 2010).

As the issue of black unwed parenthood inches into public discourse, Carroll is among the few speaking boldly about it. As a black woman who has brought thousands of babies into the world and sacrificed income to serve Houston's poor, Carroll is among the few to whom black women will actually listen. "A mama can't give it all. And neither can a daddy, not by themselves," Carroll said. "Part of the reason is because you can only give that which you have. A mother cannot give all that a man can give. A truly involved father figure offers more fullness to a child's life" (Washington 2010).

Statistics show just what that fullness means. Children of unmarried mothers of any race are more likely to perform poorly in school, go to prison, use drugs, be poor as adults, and have children out of wedlock. The black community's 72 percent rate eclipses that of most other groups: 17 percent of Asians, 29 percent of whites, 53 percent of Hispanics, and 66 percent of Native Americans were born to unwed mothers in 2008, the most recent year for which government figures are available. The rate for the overall US population was 41 percent (Washington 2010).

Abandonment/Abuse

A sense of belonging is often altered by abandonment whether real or perceived. When we desire to feel connected and cared for but are left behind and neglected, we feel abandoned. Children feel abandoned when their parents disappear from their lives, divorce, or the children experience neglect of their needs. This sense of abandonment causes the children to feel rejected and have no sense of belonging.

Fear of abandonment takes root in childhood from losing a significant relationship. For the most part, fathers are the ones who abandon their families though there has been an increasing number of mothers who have left their families due to affairs, addictions, or the desire to "find" themselves. Nevertheless, the absence of the father is critical in the development of the child as well as the sense of belonging. Also, lower self-esteem, especially among boys, and academic problems can be a common result of the absence of a father.

Boys struggle when their fathers are absent since the father provides the primary sense of belonging. One of the most reliable predictors of whether a boy will succeed or fail in school rests on a single question: Does he have a man in his life to look up to? (Tyre 2006). Too often, the answer is no. High rates of single motherhood have created a generation of fatherless boys. In every kind of neighborhood, rich or poor, an increasing number of boys—now a startling 40 percent—are being raised without their biological dads (Tyre 2006). While an uncle or a grandfather can help, psychologists emphasize that an adolescent boy without a father figure is like "an explorer without a map" (Tyre 2006, p. 50).

Even when a boy experiences discipline and correction, older males, especially fathers, can model self-restraint and solid work habits. That of course is true if the father is not an addict, not abusive, or not lazy. "An older man reminds a boy in a million different ways that school is crucial to their mission in life" (Tyre 2006, p. 51).

Statistics show the dramatic effect of fatherless boys at the college level in particular. Thirty years ago, men represented 58 percent of the undergraduate student body; now, they are a minority at 44 percent (Tyre 2006). Such numbers have profound implications for the economy, society, families, and democracy according to Margaret Spelling, a former secretary of education under President George W. Bush and president of the University of North Carolina.

Girls lose a sense of belonging, security, and love when their fathers abandon their families. They develop certain behaviors and beliefs as they grow up. Research shows that girls and young women who have unstable father figures are more liable to have an unplanned pregnancy, low self-esteem, be a high school and college dropout, and experience poverty, divorce, and sexually promiscuous behavior. One study found that:

> females without father figures often become desperate for male attention ... Females who lose their father figures to divorce or abandonment seek much more attention from men and had more physical contact with boys their age than girls from intact homes ... These females constantly seek refuge for their missing father and as a result there is a constant need to be accepted by men from whom they aggressively seek attention. (Krohn and Bogan 2001)

The authors stated that losing fathers altered their perception of men, and they may develop abandonment issues and have trouble forming lasting relationships with men (Krohn and Bogan 2001).

It is also found that a girl's academic performance may plummet due to little or no interaction with her father. Since the father provides the primary sense of belonging, a young girl can feel discouraged from pursuing a high standard. For example, Krohn and Bogan (2001) stated that fathers played a significant role in their daughter's math skills. The authors mentioned that the lack of encouragement related to academic skills could stem from feeling unprotected by their fathers, and they might feel insecure even when it came to their future education (Krohn and Bogan 2001).

The results of abandonment manifest in various ways that can actually destroy adult relationships. Adults may become possessive of all their relationships and develop codependency, dependent personality disorder, or borderline personality disorder. The *Diagnostic and Statistical Manual of Mental Disorders, Fifth Edition* (DSM-5) describes one of the various criteria of borderline personality disorder as follows.

> Individuals with borderline personality disorder make frantic efforts to avoid real or imagined abandonment. The perception of impending separation or rejection, or the loss of external structure, can lead to profound changes in self-image, affect, cognition, and behavior. These individuals are very sensitive to environmental circumstances. They experience intense abandonment fears and inappropriate anger even when faced with a realistic, time-limited separation or when there are unavoidable changes in plans. They may believe that this "abandonment" implies they are "bad." These abandonment fears are related to an intolerance of being alone and a need to have others with them. Their frantic efforts to avoid abandonment may include impulsive actions such as self-mutilating or suicidal behaviors. (DSM-5 2013, p. 663–664)

The key to freedom is recognizing the many patterns the fear of abandonment creates including a drive to always take care of others at the expense of one's own well-being. Some of these criteria describe dependency issues in the DSM-5. These drives exist because of the false belief that those who receive help from a benefactor will never leave that benefactor. Ironically, such an approach often leads to what is feared the most—more abandonment, because the person who is being smothered will in fact want relief from that.

Mental and emotional conditions based on the fear of abandonment often require long-term therapeutic treatment for such individuals. One key aspect is to reprocess the abandonment and neglect that was experienced and help people find healthy churches and ultimately the understanding that God loves them and promised, "I will never desert you, nor will I ever forsake you" (Deut. 31:6, 8; Heb. 13:5).

One of the rising diagnoses is Reactive Attachment Disorder (RAD), which is a dysfunction due to the lack of a sense of belonging. Children can act out their anger due to the disconnect and brokenness of their relationships with one or more of their parents. Abuse and abandonment repel children from relationships and cause reactions based on mistrust, which is a foundational concept of Erik Erickson, one of the leading theorists in human development. In contrast, attentiveness, instruction, and discipline can embrace children if their caregivers express a sense of love when they convey, "I love you too much to have you behave in such a negative way" (Prov. 3:11, 19:18; Heb. 12:6).

Death/Suicide

Believers in Christ are the body of Christ. When one person in the body of Christ is a victim of abuse, we are all affected. When one person in the body of Christ abuses another, we are all affected. In 1 Corinthians 12:26–27, Paul wrote, "If one part suffers, every part suffers with it; if one part is honored, every part rejoices with it. Now you are the body of Christ, and each one of you is a part of it."

The church in its first few centuries was a family that hung together through persecution, hard times, and rejection from without. The outside resistance caused the church to bond as a family and a powerful force because of its relative unity. The sense of belonging grew when there was a need to be more connected and supportive of one another.

The problem in the church in recent times has been its members distancing themselves from those who are struggling in their faith, who have been victimized, or who are experiencing divorce or broken homes. Of all places, the church needs to be where those who are broken can feel embraced through their adoption, if you will, into the group. Helping others feel they belong heals and restores them. No one has it all together, and we all need each other. However, many churches today tend to repel those who are broken and in need as if they were too different from the established group. We belong to each other.

An especially challenging situation for people is a loved one's suicide. It is often complicated grief because they face not just a loss but also the nature of the loss. Often, those who are left behind face a stigma as if they had had something to do with the suicide or should have known what signs to look for in the struggling person to suggest just a few feelings of what survivors have to deal with. The church can also do a better job of coming alongside people dealing with such complicated grief.

The following statistics from a 2013 US Center for Disease Control report provide a glimpse of the depth of the tragedy of suicide:

- About 40,000 Americans die by suicide every year.
- Suicide is the tenth leading cause of death in the United States.
- About 90 percent who die by suicide had a diagnosable mental or emotional disorder.
- Approximately twenty-two military veterans kill themselves every day—about 8,000 per year.
- One million Americans attempt suicide every year.
- Each suicide directly affects an average of six to ten survivors.
- Guns and explosives are most common methods of suicide.
- April and May are peak times for suicides.
- Suicides occur most often on Mondays and Fridays.
- Most likely times are early morning or early evening and at home. (CDC, 2013)

More than twice as many woman attempt suicide than men do, but men are more successful in completing suicide because they tend to use more-violent methods to take their lives such as hanging and fire arms. Men in particular can feel more readily disconnected when disappointments or failures arise, when relationships fail, or when they experience major health concerns.

The percentages of adults aged eighteen or older having suicidal thoughts in the previous twelve months were 2.9 percent among blacks, 3.3 percent among Asians, 3.6 percent among Hispanics, 4.1 percent among whites, 4.6 percent among Native Hawaiians / Other Pacific Islanders, 4.8 percent among American Indians/Alaska Natives, and 7.9 percent among adults reporting two or more races (SAMHSA 2014).

The desire to die is usually driven by perceived burdensomeness, hopelessness, and a sense of low belonging and social alienation.

People can feel they are burdens to others or are carrying burdens too heavy to bear. If a sense of being burdened feels overwhelming, a person may feel the only way out is suicide. Those who isolate themselves with the belief that no one is there for them can feel totally rejected by others, and that feeling can be too much to bear.

In rural areas, this sense can be exacerbated simply by the built-in aspects of greater isolation as compared to urban areas. Statics show that suicides rose in rural areas by 20 percent compared to a rise of 7 percent in metropolitan areas (CDC 2013). Wyoming had the highest rate of suicide in the nation—almost 30 deaths per 100,000 people, followed by Alaska, Montana, New Mexico, and Utah (CDC 2013). Author Bill Blackburn stated, "First, understanding suicide is a key to preventing it. Second, a close, open, personal relationship with the suicidal person is extremely important in preventing suicide" (Blackburn 1982, p. 11).

Connectedness has been viewed as the most protective mechanism against suicide. Those who sense they do not belong are subject to depression and suicidal thoughts. In his work *Man's Search for Meaning*, Viktor Frankl suggested that deep and meaningful connection to others is critical for mental, emotional, physical, and spiritual well-being (Frankl, 2014).

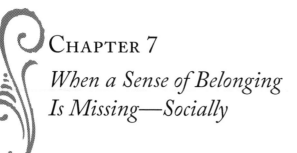

Chapter 7

When a Sense of Belonging Is Missing—Socially

Do not fear, for I am with you; do not anxiously look about you, for I am your God. I will strengthen you, surely I will help you, surely I will uphold you with My righteous right hand.

—Isaiah 41:10

The one who says he is in the Light and yet hates his brother is in the darkness until now. The one who loves his brother abides in the Light and there is no cause for stumbling in him. But the one who hates his brother is in the darkness and walks in the darkness, and does not know where he is going because the darkness has blinded his eyes.

—1 John 2:9–11

The family is the cornerstone of our sense of belonging. Without the security of knowing they are loved and accepted as a member of a family and identified as being an integral and valuable part of that family, people may try to find a sense of belonging through other means.

Some areas of society can offer a sense of belonging in the culture at large, but they are only able to partially fulfill the longing to belong. If a culture is not able to bring people a satisfying answer to their longing to belong, they will take drastic measures to belong to something or someone or risk depression that could lead to other drastic behaviors.

When a family unit is not able to provide such a stable sense of attachment, people will move to secondary alternatives such as a school community, a neighborhood community, a street gang, or a club or fraternity, which may lead them down some disappointing and even dangerous paths. For example, bullying can affect a sense of belonging (as well as safety) for a child who is on the receiving end of someone's mocking. Addictions often accompany attempts to connect with others. A strong sense of rejection can drive people to medicate the resulting pain and to seek others who are trying to do the same thing thereby forming a set of friends who seem to support one another. Street gangs, which comprise mostly boys who have decided to join such a group, provide a sense of belonging when there may be very few options of feeling connected otherwise.

Finally, though we may live in the most "connected" world that has ever existed because of electronic media, there is huge sense of loneliness instead. Social media can give people the false impression that they have many friends who sincerely care about them.

Bullying

For many children, school environments are positive learning experiences, but for many others, the school, classroom, and playground are places they may be desperate to avoid. The reason is mostly bullying. The preadolescent and adolescent years have been typically times of development and finding one's place among peers first and eventually in society. Bullying and ridicule can have an identity-altering effect on young people. The more people feel put out, pushed out, and rejected, the more they feel there is nowhere to go to find a sense of belonging.

The *Oxford American College Dictionary* (2002) defines a bully as "a person who uses strength or power to harm or intimidate those who are weaker ... typically to force him or her to do what one wants" (p. 183). Many times, bullies are not looking for their victims to do anything for them; they simply want to exert their perceived power and influence as a show of superiority. They are usually intolerant of other children who are perceived to be different, shy, weak, and unable to defend themselves. Repeated bullying can render its victims powerless to control or stop the abuse. An estimated 160,000 children miss school every day because of bullying (Newman 2013).

There are essentially four categories of bullying: physical aggression, verbal aggression, relational or social aggression, and cyberbullying, and the last category is specific to our modern era of technology and social media. Overt aggression is the physical overpowering of the victim. Examples are beating up victims, stealing their money, stealing their school lunches, or stealing items of their clothing. Verbal aggression includes name-calling, ridicule, manipulation, and threats. Relational aggression is a demand for specific compliance just to be a part of group to feed the victim's desire for belonging. Cyberbullying is using disparaging comments, images, and insults over the internet at the expense of the victim. This can humiliate the victim on a grand scale due to the vastness of the internet.

All four can have devastating effects on the victims and lead to depression, anxiety, rejection, a growing sense of loneliness, decreased self-esteem, a feeling they deserve such treatment, actually giving into the demands of the bully despite the discomfort of the demands, and in many cases suicide.

Here are some signs that a youngster is being bullied.

- Frequent headaches and stomach aches where the child says he or she can't go to school
- A reluctance to attend after-school activities
- A decline in use of phones or computers
- A drop in grades or attendance
- Changes in eating habits
- Difficulty sleeping
- Withdrawal or isolation
- Unexplained illnesses or injuries
- Self-destructive behaviors such as harming themselves, running away from home, or talk of suicide. (Newman 2013)

Bullies feel a sense of lack as well. They are often victims of bullying themselves at the hands of parents or other bullies when they were younger. Bullies have a false sense of security and even of belonging because while they may have friends, their friends are a part of their lives either out of fear of being bullied themselves, or a desire to be protected by bullies. Bullies have a false sense of community, not a real sense of belonging.

Several things can help victims of bullies. Adults can come to their defense and correct the bullies, tell them to back off, and point out that being a bully is not cool. However, while adults need to hold bullies accountable for their behavior, they should not bully bullies.

Instead, they should help them as well by offering incentives for positive behavior and determining the root of their bullying behavior such as low self-esteem, difficulties at home, and so on; bullies need a positive sense of belonging. Comfort the victims of bullying by letting them know they do not deserve to be treated that way. Encourage other children to play with those who have been bullied. If it is hard to speak up, take others with you. Don't ignore it when bullying takes place—it can stop if we all become involved.

Finally, an offshoot of bullying is prejudice. Essentially, the social roots of prejudice start with our human need to belong. We join groups, share beliefs, and social norms in large groups such as cultures down to small groups such as families. We have a natural tendency to favor those in our groups over those in other groups. Brewer (1990) suggested that prejudice may develop not because outgroups are hated but because positive emotions such as admiration, sympathy, and trust are reserved for the in group. Prejudice, whether it is due to animosity directed at different groups or because we favor those in our own groups, derives from our need to belong to groups (Cohen 2011).

Pornography

The sense of belonging can appear to exist among many who pursue substance abuse and addictions. The majority of substances abusers often do so in groups of like-minded individuals who provide what appears to be a sense of community.

In addition, a sense of belonging or perhaps more accurately a lack thereof plays into the pursuit of pornography. We were not created to be alone, and God designed sex to be enjoyed between a husband and wife. Porn leading to masturbation is a solitary act with physiological pleasure. However, in addition to the physiological pleasures that are natural to men and women, the relational component is essential for the full pleasurable experience to be enjoyed. A sense of connectedness or belonging to one another is the experience God had in mind. Lust is driven by the desire to take; love is driven by the desire to give.

The diminishing influence of fathers has left young boys with a sense of disconnectedness. Wright wrote:

> On the one hand, research overwhelmingly tells us that dads play an essential role in the lives of their sons and daughters. On the other hand, certain voices in culture not only question the necessity of dad, but insist that dads are obsolete. Just a few years ago on Father's Day, CNN featured a debate on this question: *Are some kids better off without a dad?* (Can you imagine a similar debate about motherhood on Mother's Day?). (Wright 2013)

When fathers are physically or emotionally absent, young boys in particular are left without an essential influence in their lives that would provide a strong sense of belonging. Without the sense of feeling connected to father figures, young boys may feel their self-worth lacking, and that will increase their desire to remain isolated. Isolated pursuits can be a replacement for the deficiency of a father's influence leading to pursuits of two main addictions. One is pornography, and the other is video games. One in three teenage boys is now considered a "heavy" porn user, with the average boy watching nearly two hours of porn every week (Zimbardo and Coulombe 2012).

Video games provide another escape that may satisfy the longing of feeling connected and confident. As it relates to boys' feelings of confidence, some psychologists suggest that boys measure everything they do or say by a single yardstick—whether it makes them look weak (Kindlon and Thompson 2000). That's part of the reason that videogames have such a powerful hold on boys: the action is constant, they can calibrate just how hard the challenges will be and, when they lose, the defeat is private (Tyre 2006). Also, it was found,

> Boys spend 13 hours a week playing video games, (which often include pornographic images as well as violence). As a result, boys' brains are being digitally rewired in a totally new way to demand change, novelty, excitement, and constant stimulation. That means they are becoming totally out of synch in traditional school classes, which are analog, static, and interactively passive. (Zimbardo and Coulombe 2012)

Accountability is sometimes considered a dirty word especially in addiction recovery circles. The idea, however, is founded in the need to belong. Such a need is met by having someone in your life with whom you feel comfortable enough to be transparent with and vulnerable to, a trusted friend who understands and accepts you. The sense of belonging to a person whom you feel cares enough about you to help you through struggles of overcoming addictions (or anything else for that matter) is essential in the recovery process.

Secret Societies and Gangs

Countless organizations invite individuals to be a part of something larger than themselves. Being a part of a group or an organization can indeed bring a sense of belonging and satisfaction when it relates to serving the common good. However, many organizations knowingly or unknowingly exploit the common longing to belong, but essentially, it is often more about fitting in.

Secret societies cater to the human need to belong. However, a true sense of belonging hinges on whether a person who joins such groups agrees to certain secret beliefs, rituals, and hidden truths. Alan Axelrod (1997) defined a secret society as an organization that is highly exclusive, claims to be the purveyor of special secrets, and has a membership that is strongly inclined toward one another. David V. Barrett (1999) listed these characteristics of secret societies.

- They have carefully graded and progressed teachings.
- Their teachings are available only to select individuals.
- Their teachings lead to hidden (and supposedly unique) truths.
- Their truths bring personal benefits beyond the reach and understanding of the uninitiated.

Secret societies such as Freemasonry are exclusive to their members, keep certain supposed truths from outsiders, and often through teaching and rituals promote a hierarchy of progression its members strive to attain ostensibly to improve themselves and society at large. Vanier stated,

> Secret societies and sects have a very great attraction for people who lack self-confidence or have weak personalities, because they can feel more secure when they are totally linked to others, thinking what they think, obeying without question and being manipulated into a strong sense of solidarity. (Vanier 2003, p. 21)

Secret societies pose a number of problems for Christian believers. First, the very concept of a secret society is extra-biblical at best and anti-biblical at worst. The Bible sets no precedent that encourages joining an organization marked by secrecy and hidden truths. God never commands it, and there are no examples of godly men in scripture who joined one.

Historical figures throughout post-biblical history have been members of secret societies, but many Bible verses clearly indicate the widespread, inclusive nature of the church. Several passages in scripture in particular come to mind.

- Acts 2:21—"And it shall be, that *everyone* who calls upon the name of the Lord shall be saved." (italics mine)
- Acts 10:43—"Of Him all the prophets bear witness that through His name *everyone* who believes in Him receives forgiveness of sins." (italics mine)
- Romans 10:12—"For there is no distinction between Jew and Greek; for the same Lord is Lord of all, abounding in riches for all who call upon Him."

Before joining a secret society, Christians should ask at least a couple of questions: What are they hiding? Why are they hiding it? Many resources put together by former members of secret societies can answer these questions truthfully. For example, *Kingdom of the Cults* by Walter Martin discusses various teachings including some that are secret among the various religious cults, and *The Secret Teachings of the Masonic Lodge* by Ankerberg and Weldon discusses the secret tenets of Freemasonry.

In a much less formal way, street gangs have secret beliefs and rituals distinct from those of other gangs and exclusive to only the specific gang. These gangs have been a growing phenomenon for the few decades. The Federal Bureau of Investigation (FBI) has estimated there are 1.4 million members of various kinds of street gangs comprising more than 33,000 gangs in all fifty states, the District of Columbia, and Puerto Rico. This represents a 40 percent increase from an estimated 1 million gang members in 2009 (FBI 2011).

Young people join gangs for a variety of reasons. The dangerous and sad thing about gangs is that certain people find that gangs satisfy their core longings. Of course, gangs are not a healthy way to obtain the longings and desires young boys have. Often as a result of a broken family and especially when a father is missing from the home, a young boy may feel disconnected. Other boys in the neighborhood may provide a sense of likeness and familiarity. If boys are in a formal gang, the sense of belonging to that group is even more attractive to him.

Being in a gang fulfills the need to belong, but that can lead many young people to do many unwise, dangerous, and unlawful things just to fill their longing for belonging. Children who do not feel a sense of belonging in their families will try to find it elsewhere. Some youngsters may live in well-functioning families, but if they don't believe they do, it doesn't matter how well functioning the family may be. Excessive sibling rivalry can cause that feeling even if all other family member think they belong.

Not every child is the same, nor will each child respond the same way to an inflexible approach to parenting. Parents should communicate with each of their children the uniqueness that exists in each of them. If that is not conveyed, the children can end up feeling overlooked or misunderstood rather that feeling they belong.

Being in a street gang that provides a name, a set of "colors," and interrelationships satisfies the longing of feeling connected to someone or something. Crabb commented on that mind-set:

> Our lives become thoroughly and strategically self-centered ... No one is taking care of us as we want to be taken care of, so we look after ourselves. We therefore never connect. Nothing comes out of us that is aimed at arousing the good in another. Every choice is in the service of self. We are slaves to sin. (Crabb 2005, p. 76)

First, young people need to feel part of something greater than themselves, and unfortunately, gangs often deceptively provide that. Often, young people develop a sense of pride by being identified with a gang over and above any other group. As distorted as it is, a sense of family also develops.

Second, gangs can satisfy young people's need of identity and significance. Typically, this is stronger in males than in females, but it is still an important need for both. Because teens typically struggle with who they are, they look for ways to find the answer to that. Instead of their name, family, or relationship with God, their identity is linked to a gang. Teens may find that others treat them differently because of their gang affiliation, which makes them feel important. The gang members can feel important being a part of group of like-minded individuals who have a supposedly respected (more likely a feared) name that brings significance to their identity.

Third, membership in a gang can fulfill the need for purpose. The purpose may be illegal such as drug running, gun dealing, or prostitution, but those are nonetheless purposes. Also, when a gang's turf is threatened or breached, defending it can be a purpose.

Fourth, young people can often feel that their fellow gang members understand them. Gang members often come from the same neighborhood or a similar environment, and as a result, they can relate to one another. Such an understanding can form a bond that is difficult to break. The feeling is that no one except those in the gang can see them for who they are or believe they are.

Fifth, in a deceptive way, being in a gang can address the need to feel safe and secure. This particular need is typically stronger in females than it is in males, but it is still a need for both. The individual is in a sense covered by the other gang members should he be threatened, harmed, beaten up, or swindled in a street deal of some kind. Being a part of a group of any kind brings the sense of security that is better than feeling alone. Of course, revenge is the name of the game in gangs, but that somehow provides a sense of security knowing that gang members have each other's back.

Finally, gangs provide an outlet for a young person's anger. Since one common characteristic of gangs is fighting, gang membership provides a place to direct their anger and rewards for doing so. But that only perpetuates the culture of anger, bitterness, and revenge as gangs provide a justification for such feelings. There is no room for the weakness supposedly inherent in forgiveness or reconciliation. Most gang members have come from neglectful, abusive, and abandoned circumstances and as a result feel justified in making others pay for what they have lived through.

Substance Abuse

Addictive behaviors and substance abuse are growing problems in our nation. Alcohol addiction may be the best known, but drug addiction is epidemic. Overdosing on drugs especially opioids and including heroin is now the most common cause of death for Americans under age fifty (Stetzer 2018). In 2015, opioid overdoses stole the lives of over 33,000 Americans. To put this number in perspective, opioid-related deaths outnumber car crashes and gun-related deaths in the United States (Stetzer 2018).

We also now know that this is not just an urban or suburban crisis. The rate of drug-overdose deaths in rural areas has surpassed rates in urban areas. Reports have shown that from 1999 to 2015, opioid-related deaths in rural areas have quadrupled among those between ages eighteen and twenty-five (Stetzer 2018). Because of the community nature of church fellowship, the church is positioned throughout neighborhoods and communities urban and rural alike to be both first responders and communities of hope for people struggling with opioid addictions.

Many believe this phenomenon is fueled by a spiritual crisis in America, and the faith community isn't immune to this crisis. With an estimated 2.5 million of our neighbors currently addicted to opioids or related drugs, the likelihood that there are people we do life with who are affected by this epidemic is too great to ignore (Stetzer 2018). But just like other addictive behaviors, it's their new reality, and for many, a place of hidden shame—they are too embarrassed to confess their struggles to family, friends, and especially their local church. Those who are hurting are more likely to isolate themselves than seek a community. However, the church has been designed to be a healing community in which a sense of belonging can indeed benefit wayward and lonely souls. As the opioid crisis increases, so must the response of the local church even though such ministry can be a challenge. If the Christian church has anything to offer those hurting from opioid addictions, it is hope and community.

Many churches have turned to relational ministries such as Celebrate Recovery and Narcotics Anonymous and have opened their doors to the community to offer assistance and support. Those who have walked through the demanding process of recovery will tell you that a healthy, safe community is essential to healing and long-term results. This should already be a natural part of the local churches'

DNA; if not, perhaps this could be the moment the church learns to welcome those needing to feel God's love.

These programs have been extremely effective in restoring lives, but it is not always enough. Addressing the root of opioid addiction is one of the most effective long-term solutions, and it starts in the heart. The church has a unique opportunity to be a healing place, but it must be a place that is safe, loving, understanding, and willing and is capable of seeing those struggling with addictions as not merely those being helped by a program of the church but as children of a God who loves them no matter their current condition. Of all places that exist, the church especially can find ways to bring healing and restoration by being a loving community. The trend of mental health facilities and hospitals that are being overwhelmed is already upon us, and the Christian community can be a powerful resource of healing through Christ.

Loneliness

Aloneness is a frightening, bleak, and cold feeling. However, it a common feeling among human beings perhaps as much or more today than at any other time. Throughout human history, the concept of loneliness echoed throughout literature as something to avoid. For example, John Donne (1572–1631), an English poet and clergyman in the Church of England, coined the phrase "No man is an island." Matthew Arnold (1822–1888), also an English poet, wrote, "Yes! In the sea of life enisled, with echoing straits between us thrown, dotting the shoreless watery wild, we mortal millions live alone." T. S. Eliot (1888–1965), a British essayist, publisher, and playwright, wrote in his poem "The Cocktail Party," "Hell is oneself, Hell is alone, the other figures in it merely projections. There is nothing to escape from and nothing to escape to. One is always alone."

In more contemporary times, such as in the music of the 1960s and 1970s, we hear in the 1968 song "One" sung by the musical group Three Dog Night the line, "One is the loneliest number that will ever do." In 1971, the Irish singer Gilbert O'Sullivan sang "Alone Again (Naturally)" depicting the aloneness and grief he felt being stood up at the wedding altar, feeling abandoned by God, and upon the death of his father and mother. The sense of belonging is often undermined by the poignant sense of grief or aloneness.

In the New Testament, the problem of loneliness was presented with both psychological and spiritual aspects. In Matthew 14:32–37, Jesus expressed the feeling of being alone as His disciples could not support Him while He agonized in prayer in the Garden of Gethsemane and asked His Father if there was another way besides the cross to bring redemption to humanity. The apostle Paul wrote to Timothy, "Make every effort to come to me soon; for Demas, having loved this present world, deserted me" (2 Tim. 4:9–10). Later in the same chapter, Paul wrote, "At my defense no one supported me, but all deserted me; may it not be counted against them. But the Lord stood with me, and strengthened me" (vv. 16–17).

The sense of loneliness can be rooted in low self-esteem, which is the estimate one makes of his or her own worth (Skoglund 1976). Low self-esteem will cause someone to underestimate his or her value, thereby leading to problems including depression, isolation, and negative relationships. On the other hand, those who exaggerate their self-esteem can become prideful and conceited, which often causes them to experience loneliness because no one likes to be around them. The balance is found in Romans 12:3: "For through the grace given to me I say to every man among you not to think more highly of yourself than he ought to think; but to think as to have sound judgment."

Relationships with other people are a second vital factor in the problem of loneliness (Skoglund 1976). Good, healthy self-esteem decreases the potential for loneliness. Low self-esteem can actually block the good feelings that are genuinely present in good relationships and cause people to actually reject those who show love for them. Those with low self-worth will not believe or accept compliments from others, and if they do that often enough, others will feel hurt and give up on them thereby reaffirming their perceived loneliness.

Self-esteem cannot be built or rebuilt in a vacuum. It is essential that it be built in conjunction with others in relationships. A loving and devoted relationship can do wonders to heal hurt and rebuild a sense of self-worth. The strength of someone's self-esteem largely determines the kind of relationships he or she develops—the stronger the person, the stronger and healthier the friends he or she will choose (Skoglund 1976).

The Bible encourages the connectivity of one another to overcome loneliness. In 1 Corinthians 12:12–27, Paul emphasized the body of Christ—the church and the vast company of believers. The passage says that we all need each other, that each member has different gifts to use and thus contribute to the community, and that all belong equally to each other. For example, we read, "But now there are many members, but one body. And the eye cannot say to the hand, 'I have no need of you'; or again the head to the feet, 'I have no need of you'" (1 Cor. 12:20–21).

Ultimately, our loneliness is overcome by relationship with God through Jesus Christ. We all were made for fellowship first with God and then with each other. Saint Augustine wrote, "Thou hast made us for thyself, O Lord, and our heart is restless until it finds its rest in thee" (*Confessions of Augustine*). Colossians 2:9–10 states: "For in

Him [Jesus] all the fullness of deity dwells in bodily form, and in Him you have been made complete."

Skoglund suggested some helpful steps that can alleviate the sense of loneliness.

- Live in a way that makes you proud of yourself (in a healthy, balanced way).
- Do things that create self-respect.
- Reach out to help others in need.
- Form relationships with people who make you feel worthwhile.
- Seek professional help if your loneliness and low self-esteem seem too profound or if they don't respond to your genuine efforts to overcome them.
- Don't feel guilty if as a Christian you experience loneliness; that's part of being human. There can be legitimate reasons, but don't ignore them. Seek out a trusted friend.
- Try to maintain a daily attitude of commitment to God. (Be ever so mindful that He is with you in every present moment). (Skoglund 1976)

CHAPTER 8

The Ultimate Sense of Belonging

Do not fear, for I have redeemed you; I have called you by name; you are Mine! When you pass through the waters, I will be with you; and through the rivers they will not overflow you. When you walk through the fire, you will not be scorched, nor will the flame burn you.

—Isaiah 43:1–2

For this very night an angel of the God to whom I belong and whom I serve stood before me.

—Acts 27:23

A man can receive only what is given him from heaven.

—John 3:27

No matter how we may avoid this important truth, life is relational. We were created in relationship, through relationship, and for relationship. Without the reality and reciprocity of relationships, life itself would not exist or continue. But because we live in a fallen, imperfect world, healthy relationships are rarely simple or easy. Much of the brokenness we experience in our lives is due to some form of broken, abusive, or dysfunctional relationship. And sometimes even in such relationships, the strong desire to belong keeps us in harmful relationships because at least we feel attached to others as destructive as that can be.

There is a brief scene and dialog from the 2015 Star Wars movie *The Force Awakens* between the character Matz and the lead character Rey.

MATZ: Dear Child, I see your eyes. You already know the truth—whoever you are waiting for on Jakku—they're never coming back … But, there's someone who still could.

REY: (*speaking softly*) Luke?

MATZ: The belonging you seek is not behind you—it is ahead!

A sense of belonging can be found again if you have had it missing in your life. In my experience with people, I agree with Vanier, who stated, "There are so many who are looking for a sense of belonging and a meaning to their lives" (Vanier 1989, p. 283). Your past may have included your or your parents' divorce, the death of a parent, never knowing your father, neglect, or abuse. Any of these experiences and more could communicate to youngsters especially, but also to adults, that they did not belong or that someone had rejected them. Vanier observed, "It is obvious that too much solitude can drive people off the rails, to depression or alcoholism. More and more people seem to have lost their balance because their family life has been unhappy" (Vanier 1989, p. 283).

While life experiences can indeed contribute to a sense of

brokenness, I have found in working with broken and wounded people that their *interpretation* of what they experienced can also be problematic. What they believed to have been behind someone's actions could have been the source of their feelings of rejection. I often help people process through not just the actions of others who have offended or hurt them but also their own belief systems that usually have developed as a result of actions.

As I briefly discussed in a previous chapter, the theorists in the field of psychology all had various impactful experiences that contributed to their views of the human condition and human development. Essentially, they were looking for ways to provide answers to the broken human condition and why people feel the way they do and the way they behave. The reason is that all human development occurs through attachment to others, a belonging or connectedness to others, or the lack thereof.

Humankind has been looking for answers ever since Adam and Eve rebelled. Humans have been seeking answers from broken people, through and in broken thinking, and from this broken world. As long as we live with these feelings, based on our past, we will continue to be stuck in a sense of disconnectedness. And as long as we look to a broken world for our sense of belonging, our sense of belonging will also remain less satisfying and broken.

But there is hope. The hope is in the present, and as a result, it can be translated to the future. The hope is knowing that we belong to God, who created us. Even if we sense a huge chasm between ourselves and God, He made a way of restoration. He bought us back! Jesus made it possible to experience being reconnected with our Father, who loves us dearly and longs for relationship with us. Johnson wrote:

> Both attachment science and Christianity teach that
> turning to others and acknowledging our vulnerability is
> admirable, and that responding with empathy and care to
> others is a key part of emotional and spiritual wholeness.
> (Johnson 2016, 28)

Jesus promised to never leave us or forsake us: "I am with you always, even to the end of the age" (Matt. 28:20).

God made the Garden of Eden a place of peace and provision for humanity. Adam and Eve had it all, most important, an unbroken, intimate relationship with their Creator and the lover of their souls. Adam and Eve enjoyed perfect peace and provision as they served God and one another. After the six days of creation, God said that things were good and very good (Gen. 1:10, 12, 18, 21, 25, 31). The only caveat was that God acknowledged that it was not good for man to be alone (Gen. 2:18). This speaks to the first core longing in human beings—a sense of belonging. The basic question of this core longing is to whom or what we belong. Adam belonged to God, and God belonged to Adam. That was established and was not in question at the time.

However, as mentioned earlier, God knew that Adam needed to relate to someone who was suitable for him and who was of like kind (Gen. 2:20). After naming all the animals, Adam evidently discovered he had no one like him with whom to relate. All humans are created and "hard wired" to be attached to someone and something. God created in marriage the primary relationship to satisfy the sense of belonging. When a husband and wife feel connected, in love, in good communication, knowing and trying to meet each other's needs, and showing mutual respect and preference towards each other, a sense of belonging to each other grows stronger and more satisfying. The accompanying result is often a sense of identity.

Adam's words after seeing Eve were poignant. Genesis 2:23-24 records Adam's reaction:

> And the man said, "This is now bone of my bones, and flesh of my flesh; She shall be called Woman, because she was taken out of Man." For this cause a man shall leave his father and mother, and shall cleave to his wife; and they shall become one flesh.

Eve belonged to Adam and Adam belonged to Eve because they were totally connected through body, mind, and spirit. Their identities were intricately compatible and connected to one another through love. They both ultimately belonged to God. Their being was ultimately defined in God. However, they also felt a sense of belonging to each other. This was God's design for mankind in general, and specifically, men and women in marriage. This is the essence of family, which is the foundation to every human culture and relationship: to know where we belong and to whom. Cahn wrote:

> We were each created to be the bride. That's why we can never be complete in ourselves. That's why deep down, in the center of our being, in the deepest part of our heart, we seek to be filled. For the bride is made to be married. So we can never find our completion until we are joined to Him who is beyond us. And that is why we go through our lives trying to join ourselves to that which we think will fill the longing in our hearts—to people, success, possessions, achievements, money, comfort, acceptance, beauty, romance, family, power, a movement, a goal, and any multitude of things. (Cahn 2016, p. 14)

As a result, we all need a Bridegroom to complete us. The only Bridegroom who can complete us in the way we need is Jesus. To fully belong to Him would be like marrying God in the Spirit. The Bible calls us the bride of Christ, and as such, we belong to Him. Nothing is more intimate with a true sense of belonging as understanding that God has chosen us to be in relationship with Him. Cahn added:

> By joining every part of your life and being—your deepest parts, your heart, your soul, your wounds, your longings, your desires, everything—to God. Only then can you be complete. Only then can your deepest needs and longings be fulfilled ... And the bride can only find her completion in the Bridegroom. And the Bridegroom of our souls ... is God. (Cahn 2016, p. 14)

Attachment theory can also be applied to how we connect with God. It is important to see how the different attachment styles play out as they relate to relationship with God. Because God functions more similarly to the parent-child relationship, the importance of our family environment truly affects the way we become attached to God, if we attach to Him at all.

For example, avoidance attachment individuals show a reluctance to communicate with God, show obsessive self-reliance, and avoid emotionality in their relationship with God. Avoidant people are more likely to turn to worldly things or idols to calm them down and bring meaning to their lives. After all, in their minds, God is a distant, uncaring power, and avoidant people believe they can do better dealing with their lives than can God. Avoidant individuals may have the intellectual capacity to love, but they lack the emotional capacity to do so.

Anxious attachment people have a preoccupation and worry about their relationship with God as if God will eventually abandon them. They constantly go to the altar, and they feel they are only as good as their last encounter with God. As soon as something bad happens, they feel God is abandoning them and does not love them because they are not worthy of love. Often as a result, anxious attachment people are more likely to turn to earthly relationships as unhealthy and destructive as they may be as their idols. An essential part of codependency is when people feel they can find value only in another person. They also tend to be jealous of others who seem to have God's favor over them. They are concerned about whether they are lovable enough for God, and they feel resentment toward God when things don't go as they expect they should.

One well-known New Testament story clearly illustrates anxious attachment—the story of the Prodigal Son in Luke 15:11–32. While many people are familiar with the story especially as it relates to the wayward son who eventually came to his senses (v. 17), the older son is often overlooked. After the younger son returned home humbled and broken, the father was so happy that he ordered a feast to celebrate his son's return.

The older son became quite angry and indignant over such a party (v. 28) and complained to his father that the younger son did not deserve such treatment because of his behavior. He said, "Look! For many years I have been serving you, and I have never neglected a command of yours; and yet you have never given me a young goat, that I might be merry with my friends" (v. 29). The father responded, "My child, you have been with me, and all that is mine is yours" (v. 31). The father's message was that his older son's belonging to the father was never in question and that he had no need to feel envious. All he had to have done was ask and who he was would have been celebrated too.

Secure attachment people feel secure in their relationship with God and relate to Him well. People who grow up securely attached to primary caregivers are more likely to sustain a future belief and relationship with God. In the midst of challenging and disappointing experiences, secure people will still find solace in God, and their relationship with God will become stronger. Envy does not exist since secure people already humbly realize they are blessed beyond measure, and they do not resort to comparison games.

In a previous chapter, I discussed the concept of fitting in versus belonging. I mentioned that when we lose ourselves in a group or to another person, we are fitting in, not belonging. "When you love your friends for what they can do for you, you will soon be impatient, jealous, and mistrustful" (Fenelon 1992). But there is one exception: Jesus said, "He who has lost his life for my sake shall find it" (Matt. 10:39, 16:25). Was Jesus asking us to become codependent? Was He contradicting His teaching by suggesting such a thing? Of course not. Jesus often taught in contrasts and in parables. The truth is that we all need to be dependent on God and accountable to Him for our lives. But such dependency does not cause us to lose ourselves; rather, we gain ourselves by belonging to God. Jesus declared in Luke 9:24–25, "For whoever wishes to save his life shall lose it, but whoever loses his life for My sake, he is the one who will save it. For what is a man profited if he gains the world, and loses or forfeits himself?"

When we are forced to fit in for the sake of others or a group, we benefit nothing from the arrangement except for the deceived feeling that we belong and are valued. Jesus was teaching us that when we lose what we believe to be our lives—our sinful, self-centered, worldly, rebellious lives—we will find true life and our true selves. We regain what Jesus restored for us—our true selves.

As I discussed in my book *Created for Significance*, we all have experienced identity theft. Our sense of belonging to the Almighty God has been severed by sin and rebellion. As a result, we all try to fit in somewhere and somehow by our own power and understanding. In doing so, we all miss the mark. We all miss the best God has to offer us.

The alternative is to surrender our lives to Jesus not to lose who we truly are but to allow God to restore us to who we were supposed to be. Galatians 4:4–9 declares:

> But when the fullness of the time came, God sent forth His Son, born of a woman, born under the Law, in order that he might redeem those who were under the Law, that we might receive the adoption as sons. And because you are sons, God has sent forth the Spirit of His Son into our hearts, crying, "Abba! Father!" Therefore, you are no longer a slave, but a son; and if a son, then an heir through God. However, at that time, when you did not know God, you were slaves to those which by nature are no gods. But now that you have come to know God, or rather to be known by God, how is it that you turn back again to the weak and worthless elemental things, to which you desire to be enslaved all over again?

Crabb added:

> Until we realize that there are no legitimate longings in our souls beyond His power and intention to satisfy, all change is cosmetic. But as we grasp how tenderly committed He is to our well-being, we feel more inclined to obey. Good urges become stronger. (Crabb 2005, 14)

When we experience relationship with the lover of our souls and truly know Him as the good Father He is, our desires change to wanting to obey and follow Him, to be a blessing to others, and to make an impact wherever we are. It is not that we need to do good to obtain a belonging to God, rather, a sense of belonging to God actually empowers us to seek and do good.

People tend to seek God whenever they experience a crisis, a need for His intervention, or in times of disappointment. Others may actually turn from God in similar situations. What is clear is that belonging to God and knowing we belong to Him has a tremendous effect on how we deal with life and the problems it brings. Johnson observed:

> For the Christian, however, God is not simply a bastion of hope and confidence when facing distress and danger, or even a resource that empowers us to explore and engage with our world. Understanding the power of secure attachment shows us how trust in God, the ultimate attachment figure, can be a powerful source of positive fulfillment and personal growth throughout life. Those who know and live with a sense of secure connection to special loved ones have been shown to be more able to tune in to and be compassionate toward others, deal with anger constructively, cope with distress, stay open to and forgive others, show more generosity and tolerance, and shape a positive sense of self as one who is worthy of love and care. (Johnson 2016, p. 255–256)

Today, the American church is splintered. There are Caucasian churches, Hispanic churches, and Black churches. There are mainline denominational churches and independent churches. Some churches cater to the young using modern means such as multimedia, and other churches are more traditional. Some churches conduct traditional worship using hymns and liturgy, and others use entirely contemporary music often in concert-like environments. There are seeker churches and strong, doctrinal churches.

The good news about the above descriptions is that just about anyone can find a church that may fit him or her. The bad news is that many churches in their approaches are trying to fit into the current culture rather than be a factor for change in the culture. And the commitment to discipleship, which is a measure that indicates to whom we belong, is lacking as well. Hebrews 10:24–25 states:

> And let us consider how to stimulate one another to love and good deeds, not forsaking our own assembling together, as is the habit of some, but encourage one another; and all the more, as you see the day drawing near.

Ultimately, we belong to God's kingdom and to His church through Jesus Christ. If we make the church too much in our image or in the image of our culture, we are not really belonging to God's family. Instead, we are trying to get the church to fit in, and as a result, we may really not feel we belong to the real church of Christ but rather to a cultural, watered-down version of true connection with God through Jesus Christ.

The church of Jesus Christ should include the young, the old, whites, and minority groups worshipping together in a mix of traditional approaches with contemporary aspects that are meaningful with substantive teachings and life applications and in fresh approaches that can be helpful in presenting a sense of belonging, not simply fitting in. Crabb suggested:

I want to encourage older Christians to believe they have something wonderful to give that only years can supply; I want to see them enter meaningfully into the lives of younger people and be well received as their elders, their shepherds, their spiritual guides. And I want to see them honored for doing so. (Crabb 2005, p. 82)

James made clear what God was seeking:

This is pure and undefiled religion in the sight of our God and Father, to visit orphans (the fatherless; to provide belonging) and widows (to provide belonging and covering) in their distress, and to keep oneself unstained by the world" (James 1:27; additions mine).

The Old Testament prophet Hosea declared an appeal to the people of God that is still timely:

Return, O Israel, to the Lord your God, for you have stumbled because of your iniquity. Take words with you and return to the Lord. Say to Him, "Take away all iniquity, and receive us graciously, that we may present the fruit of our lips. Assyria will not save us, we will not ride on horses; nor will we say again, Our god, to the work of our hands; for in Thee the fatherless finds mercy." (Hosea 14:1–3)

The answer may be complicated, but the solution is the one gospel, not many, that brings life. The apostle Paul wrote:

There is one body and one Spirit, just as also you were
called in one hope of your calling; one Lord, one faith,
one baptism, one God and Father of all who is over all and
through all and in all" (Eph. 4:4–6).

In summary, attachment theories can be brought together with
the empowering truth of the Word of God. Johnson suggested, "The
first principle of attachment science is that we all have a built-in
longing for connection with someone who will respond to us and
keep us safe" (Johnson 2016, p. 251). This longing is not for abstract
concepts such as knowledge, possessions, or power. If we are all
honest with ourselves, it is for a felt sense of belonging. We are born
helpless and stay that way longer than any other animal on this planet
(Johnson 2016).

We can feel we belong as we become connected to another we
know loves us and whom we trust. Perhaps most of us become aware
of the longing for belonging when it is not being met. Henri Nouwen
wrote:

The mystery of God's presence can be touched only by a
deep awareness of His absence. It is in the center of our
longing for the absent God that we discover His footprints
and realize that our desire to love God is born out of the
love with which He has touched us. (Nouwen 2005)

Ultimately, such a sense is one of connection to our loving,
heavenly Father. Jeremiah 29:13 states, "You will seek me and find
me when you seek me with all you heart."

The second aspect of attachment theory that is congruent with Christian principles is that it offers people a safe place to be—a place of peace, comfort, and consolation. This principle I discuss in my second book in this series, *Created for Covering*. A person's sense of safety is huge in developing meaningful relationships. From the needs of the infant to those of a senior citizen, the need for safety in attachment is essential in order to feel the sense of belonging is secure and positive. "Anxiety in the heart of a man weighs it down, but a good word makes it glad" (Prov. 12:25).

The third aspect of attachment or a secure sense of belonging is that it makes us stronger. When we feel secure and attached to a healthy caregiver and a healthy environment, that frees us to explore, create, be confident in other environments, grow, and feel empowered. We are able to thrive, be resilient, and know we can return to our safe havens and be recharged to go try again. That is an invaluable asset and experience for anyone. Psalm 138:3 states, "On the day I called Thou didst answer me; Thou didst make me bold with strength in my soul." In Psalm 18:2, God was described as "my rock and my fortress." In Psalm 27:1, God was "the strength of my life."

The fourth attachment aspect is a negative one. When we lose the sense of belonging, it profoundly hurts. Johnson stated:

> When love doesn't work, we hurt. Indeed, "hurt feelings" is a precisely accurate phrase, according to psychologist Naomi Eisenberg of the University of California. Her brain imagining studies show that that rejection and exclusion trigger the same circuits in the same part of the brain, the anterior cingulate, as physical pain. In fact, this part of the brain turns on anytime we are emotionally separated from those who are close to us. When I read this study, I

remembered being shocked by my own physical experience of grief. After hearing that my mother had died, I felt battered, like I had literally been hit by a truck. And when we are close to, hold, or make love with our partners, we are flooded with the "cuddle hormones" oxytocin and vasopressin. These hormones seem to turn on "reward" centers in the brain, flooding us with calm and happiness chemicals like dopamine, and turning off the stress hormones like cortisol. (Johnson 2016, p. 36)

Even Jesus experienced deep visceral grief and anxiety as He was hanging on the cross. In Matthew 27:46, He cried out, "My God, my God, why have you forsaken me?"

To feel alone is perhaps one of the most powerful and tragic experiences we can have especially if rejection is involved. It's because we were not created to be alone but to belong. Clinton and Straub wrote:

It's said that kids really aren't afraid of the dark ... they're afraid of being alone in the dark. Big kids are the same way, especially in the darkness of life. Whether we admit or not, we all want to belong. We also crave to know that if we died today, somebody would care. That's because we were made for relationships. To love and be loved. When we're left alone and to ourselves, our hearts eventually grow cold over time as we drift into depression and apathy. And slowly but surely, we die. At least inside. (Clinton and Straub 2010)

We were created to belong and interact with each other in positive, beneficial ways. The Bible exhorts us all to connect. There are fifty-nine "one another" statements in the New Testament—fifty-nine exhortations in scripture to actually do something toward others. These are behaviors we may do out of an overflow of our relationship with Jesus, but they are not things we do solely for Jesus; others must be involved in order to fulfill them. For example, Romans 12:10 says, "Be devoted to one another in brotherly love; give preference to one another in honor." A sense of belonging includes devotion to one another, and it will breed respect and honor for all involved.

Peter wrote, "Be hospitable to one another without complaint. As each one has received a special gift, employ it in serving one another, as good stewards of the manifold grace of God" (1 Pet. 4:9-10). We can all help others feel connected and valued by being blessings to them when we show hospitality and give of our time and resources. After all, we are simply stewards or managers of what we have since everything belongs to God.

Finally, God promises healing to those who ask for it. James 5:16 states, "Confess your sins to each other and pray for each other so that you may be healed." Healing requires connection, a humble spirit, and admission of our sins. Only a true, positive sense of belonging can bring healing, forgiveness, restoration, encouragement, meaningfulness, understanding, significance, and connectedness for all involved.

To Whom We Ultimately Belong

In our American culture, we increasingly hear people declare that they have rights and that what they have or are entitled to have should be afforded to them. After all, we are supposed to have the rights to life, liberty, and the pursuit of happiness. One problem is that the way it is worded, most people feel that happiness is a goal and is their right. In truth, happiness is not a *goal* that can be obtained like riches—it's a *result* of lives well lived. Besides, if we understand the role of Adam and Eve and humankind from the very beginning, we see that God gave us the responsibility—not the right—to be stewards of His creation.

Essentially, God is still Creator and owns everything. He has simply delegated to us to be responsible for all that He created and good stewards of what is actually His. Because we are His creation, we also belong to Him unless sin, the flesh, or the devil has captured us and led us away. The good news, the essential message of the gospel, is that God provided a way to bring us back to Him. He sent Jesus Christ to defeat the world system, the power of sin and the flesh, Satan himself, and even death. The resurrection defeated these all.

First, Deuteronomy 10:14 declares, "To the Lord your God belong heaven and the highest heavens, the earth and all that is in it." Everything belongs to God and rightly so since He created everything as Genesis 1–2 describes. God simply placed His creation in the hands of Adam and Eve as stewards, responsible mangers, of what truly belonged to Him.

Second, Job 41:11 quotes God speaking to Job: "Whatever is under the whole heaven is Mine." Jeremiah 27:5 makes a similar declaration with the added statement "I have made the earth, the men and the beasts which are on the face of the earth by My great power and by My outstretched arm, and I will give it to the one who is pleasing in My sight." Here as in Genesis 1:28–30, God made it clear that He was giving the earth and everything in it to humankind not to keep but to be responsible stewards of it. The Hebrew word *nathan* used here and in most of the Old Testament means "ascribe," "appoint," "to be in charge of," and "to bring forth." Ultimately, the only rights we have are what God has bestowed on us. We essentially do not own anything, we are simply stewards. Everything belongs to Him, including you and me.

Our mind-set should always be that whatever we have has ultimately come from God and that we are simply managers of what we have been given. Such a mind-set is often foreign to the current paradigm of many people who believe they deserve whatever they want. That mind-set also includes the sense of demanding to be treated special. The sad part about this conflict is that God desires to indeed lavish everything on those He loves and delights, and He desires the success of us all. The problem becomes when we choose not believe the heart of God and as a result take for ourselves and demand our "rights."

Christians are often guilty of a similar attitude as it relates to what belongs to God. We often speak about "our" ministry, spiritual gifts, worship, or teachings. While there are many aspects to the church and its ministries, the apostle Paul made clear what was the source of all things related to the church in 1 Corinthians 12:4–7:

> Now there are a variety of gifts, but the same Spirit, and there are a variety of ministries, and the same Lord. And there are varieties of effects, but the same God who works all things in all person. But to each one is *given* the manifestation of the Spirit for the common good ... But one and the same Spirit works all these things, *distributing* to each one individually just as *He wills*. (italics mine)

The gifts of the Spirit are God's to give. The connotation to give in Greek means to have power or to manifest something God chooses to reveal through a person yet it remains God's power. The gifts manifested still belong to God, who chooses to use people to bless people.

Many of us say that "my church" is the one on the corner, or the one that has the tall steeple, or the one known for reaching out to the community and so on. In fact, it is not even the churches to which we belong though it is a common and acceptable way to describe the churches we attend. After the apostle Peter made his declaration that Jesus was "the Christ, the son of the living God" (Matt. 16:16), Jesus said, "And I say to you that you are Peter, and upon this rock I will build *My* church; and the gates of Hades shall not overpower it" (Matt. 16:18; italics mine). Paul added to the understanding in 1 Corinthians 12:27 in which he described the functions in the church of the many distinct members and called the church "the body of Christ."

I have heard many suggest that when they teach, they are presenting their own teachings, yet as we are coming to understand, all knowledge and teaching belong to God. Jesus said even His teaching came from the Father. Many marveled at Jesus's words and knowledge because they perceived Him as unlearned, and in response, He declared, "My teaching is not Mine, but His who sent me" (John 7:15–16).

Later, Jesus assured His disciples that they too would be able to enunciate the teachings of the gospel, but He reminded them where they would ultimately receive such preparation. John 14:26 quoted Jesus: "But the Helper, the Holy Spirit, whom the Father will send in My name, *He will teach you all things*, and bring to your remembrance all that I said to you" (italics mine).

Ultimately, the salvation that is given to us is God's salvation, not ours. Psalm 9:14 states, "That I may tell of all Thy praises, that … I may rejoice in Thy salvation." In one the most humble prayers that any of us can express, David made it clear to whom we should pray.

> Create in me a clean heart O God, and renew a steadfast
> spirit within me. Do not cast me away from *Thy* presence,

and do not take *Thy* Holy Spirit from me. Restore unto me
the joy of *Thy* salvation, and sustain me with a willing spirit.
(Ps. 51:10–12; italics mine)

It is clear that we can be in God's presence—His Holy Spirit—
and our salvation is really His salvation that He grants to those who
accept Jesus Christ.

One of the cultural buzzwords is being "spiritual." The connotation
is that human beings can be spiritual and that by virtue of that can
determine their own salvation. We often think that we can save
ourselves or heal ourselves or that we have enough strength to do
this or that. No one can do all things, but "I can do all things
through Him who strengthens me" (Phil. 4:13). The power to do
ultimately comes from the One who created us, knows us, loves us,
and empowers us—Jesus Christ. Psalm 110:3 declares that God's
power moves people to do good and help others. Our lives are not
our own; they belongs to the One who created and sustains life.

Daniel 2:22 says, "It is He who *reveals* the profound and hidden
things; He knows what is in the darkness, and the light dwells with
Him. In the New Testament we read, "Every good thing *given* and
every perfect gift is from above, coming down from the Father of
lights, with whom there is no variation or shifting shadow" (James
1:17). John states, "A man can receive only what is *given* him from
heaven" (John 3:27). If only we could develop a mind-set like that
of John the Baptist, who declared, "He must increase, but I must
decrease" (John 3:30), the church would become more effective.

There are many other things that belong to God, and the way we
use them can bless or curse God and ourselves. For example, God's
name is sacred; He made it clear that we were not to use His name in
vain; Exodus 20:7 states, "You shall not take the Name of the Lord

your God in vain, for the Lord will not leave him unpunished who takes *His* name in vain" (italics mine). Isaiah 43:7 adds, "Everyone who is called by *My* name, and whom I have created for *My* glory, whom I have formed, even whom I have made" (italics mine).

Other examples are these:

- My commandments—Ex. 20:6; 1 John 5:3
- My covenant—Ps. 25:14; Mal. 2:4–5
- My Word—Ps. 119:105; John 14:15, 23
- My people—Isa. 40:1; Jer. 30:22; Hos. 4:6; 1 Chron. 7:14; Rev. 18:1–4
- My will (or the will of God)—Jer. 29:11; John 7:17; 1 Thess. 4:3; 1 Pet. 2:15
- My name—Matt. 10:22, 18:20
- My Father (Jesus said)—John 14:23
- My Son—Ps. 2:7; Matt. 16:13–17; John 20:30–31; 1 John 5:9–13
- My Spirit; the Spirit of God—Luke 4:18, 11:13; Acts 2:17; Rom. 8:9; Eph. 4:30
- My throne—Isa. 66:1; Matt. 5:34, 23:22; Acts 7:49; Rev. 3:21
- My church—Matt. 16:18
- My house—Matt. 21:13
- My messenger (referring to John the Baptist, but all servants of God are not autonomous)—Matt. 11:10
- My body and blood—Matt. 26:26–28
- My money (our gratitude relies on the concept that all things belong to God)—Matt. 25:27
- My yoke and My burden (we do not carry our troubles alone; they can be given to Jesus)—Matt. 11:30

- My glory—Isa. 42:8, 43:7; Phil. 4:19; John 1:14; 2 Cor. 4:6; Heb. 1:3
- My grace—2 Cor. 12:9
- Life in general (we ultimately belong to God)—Isa. 43:1; Matt. 10:39, 16:25

Psalm 139:6–15 reads:

> Such knowledge is too wonderful for me; it is too high, I cannot attain to it. Where can I go from *Your* Spirit? Or where can I flee from *Your* presence? If I ascend to heaven, You are there; If I make my bed in Sheol, behold, You are there. If I take the wings of the dawn, if I dwell in the remotest part of the sea, even there *Your* hand will lead me, and *Your* right hand will lay hold of me. If I say, "Surely the darkness will overwhelm me, and the light around me will be night," even the darkness is not dark to You, and the night is as bright as the day. Darkness and light are alike to You. For You formed my inward parts; You wove me in my mother's womb. I will give thanks to You, for I am fearfully and wonderfully made; Wonderful are Your works, And my soul knows it very well. My frame was not hidden from You, when I was made in secret. (italics mine)

Remember, you belong to Jesus. He is waiting for you to accept Him into your life for healing, restoration, and relationship. Because we are all broken people, we need the Redeemer who can heal, take away the stain and effect of sin and evil in our lives, and restore us to right relationship to God, our Creator, and to other people. Once we accept the loving and gracious embrace of Jesus, we can develop meaningful connections with others who can provide encouragement and edification to our lives.

Join a solid church that is not conforming to the culture but is impacting the culture with strong insightful biblical teaching and with like-minded, connected people. Perhaps find a mentor who can positively speak into your life and provide some meaningful direction. Also, consider a Christian counselor if you have unresolved hurts that prevent you from developing healthy relationships and thus face your longings in a positive way. No one can go it alone.

So to where do you ultimately belong? Here are some summarized conclusions:

- to the Name above all names (Phil. 2:9)
- to a God who created you (Ps. 139:13)
- to a God who has a plan for you (Jer. 29:11)
- to a God who delights in you (Zeph. 3:17)
- to a God who is your strong tower (Prov. 18:10)
- to a God in whom you can do all things (Phil. 4:13)
- to a God who is greater than anyone in the world (1 John 4:4)
- to a kingdom and a name that have no end (Isa. 9:7; Luke 1:33)

Ultimately, everything belongs to God, and thankfully, we belong to God as well. If we could frame that in the manner whereby we realize that the Creator of the universe is actually intimately interested in us all in a personal way, we can be so thankful that we belong to the Creator of the universe. If we think about that, nothing we belong to such as a team, club, college, city, vocation, relationship, church, or even our family can ever compare with knowing we belong to God, and He gladly embraces us and causes us to feel connected to

Him through Jesus Christ. Paul declared, "More than that, I count all things to be loss in view of the surpassing value of knowing Christ Jesus my Lord, for whom I have suffered the loss of all things, and count them but rubbish so that I may gain Christ" (Phil. 3:8).

During his life with Jesus, Peter learned many things about dependence as well as freedom and where He belonged and to whom; he said, "His divine power has given us everything we need for life and godliness through the knowledge of Him who called us by His own glory and excellence" (2 Peter 1:3). This from the man who had a poignant response to Jesus's question "You do not want to go away also, do you?" At that time, Peter declared, "Lord, to whom shall we go? You have words of eternal life" (John 6:67–68). That is the response God seeks from us for our benefit knowing that belonging to Him will bring out the best in us, the strength in us, and the life in us.

To know who we are, to feel safe, secure, and covered, to be encouraged in our purpose, to understand God and feel understood and take the time to understand others, and to feel a sense of belonging that we all need, we must know we are loved and can freely express our love one to another. "Love means letting others reach us and becoming sensitive enough to reach them. The cement of unity is interdependence" (Vanier 1989, 48).

Love, the theme of the next and last book in this series, discusses the foundation of love, the source of love, the aspects of love, and love busters as well as love builders one with another. As I have mentioned throughout this series, all six of these core longings, while addressed separately for clarification purposes, are eternally intertwined and interdependent on each other. Perhaps the strongest longing, love, is the beginning and the end of linking all these core longings together. After all, the Bible says God is love (1 John 4:7–8).

APPENDIX

Discovering Your Attachment Style

Below is a personal assessment tool that will help you discover your attachment style. This is simply a tool to assist you in helping you see what may be your attachment style. It is important to note that your attachment style can change depending on the specific relationships you are in as it appears more readily in intimate relationships such as those with close friends and romantic relationships.

Your style may change as your relationship changes and based on how much the Lord Jesus has healed your brokenness and transformed you into more of His likeness and your true self.

As you take this survey and as you read the statements, consider how you honestly and typically feel and relate to people with whom you are in relationship. It is tempting to answer these statements according to how you would like to relate to people rather than how you actually do relate. So be honest as you go and try not to overthink the statements.

Under each attachment style section, circle the numbers next to the statements that generally describe you. Go with your first instinct, which is usually the most accurate.

Attachment Style A

1. I don't like sharing my feelings with others.
2. I don't like it when my partner wants to talk about his or her feelings.
3. I have a hard time understanding how others feel.
4. When I get stressed, I try to deal with the situation by myself.
5. My partner often complains that I don't like to talk about how I feel.
6. I don't really need close relationships.
7. I highly value my independence and self-sufficiency.
8. I don't worry about being alone or abandoned.
9. I don't worry about being accepted by others.
10. I tend to value personal achievements and success over close, intimate relationships.

Attachment Style B

1. I really like sharing my feelings with my partner, but he or she does not seem as open as I am.
2. My feelings can often get out of control pretty quickly.
3. I worry about being alone.
4. I worry about being abandoned in close relationships.
5. My partner complains that I am too clingy and too emotional.
6. I strongly desire to be very intimate with people.
7. In my closest relationships, the other person doesn't seem as desirous of intimacy and closeness as I am.
8. I worry a great deal about being rejected by others.

9. I tend to value close, intimate relationships over personal achievement and success.

10. When I get stressed, I desperately seek others for support, but others do not seem as available as I would like them to be.

Attachment Style C

1. My feelings are very confusing to me, so I try not to feel them.

2. My feelings can be very intense and overwhelming.

3. I feel torn between wanting to be close to others and wanting to pull away from them.

4. My partner complains that sometimes I'm really needy and clingy and other times I'm distant and aloof.

5. I have a difficult time letting others get close to me, but once I let them in, I worry about being abandoned or rejected.

6. I feel very vulnerable in close relationships.

7. Sometimes, I feel very disconnected from myself and my feelings.

8. I can't decide whether or not I want to be in close relationships.

9. Other people can really hurt me if I let them get too close.

10. Close relationships are difficult to come by because people are always unpredictable in their actions and behaviors.

Attachment Style D

1. I find it easy to share my feelings with people I'm close to.

2. I like it when my partner wants to share his or her feelings with me.

3. I am comfortable getting close to others, but I also feel comfortable being alone.

4. I expect my partner to respect who I am.

5. I expect my partner to respond to my needs in a sensitive and appropriate way.
6. Building intimacy in relationships comes relatively easy for me.
7. I let myself feel my emotions, but I'm rarely if ever overwhelmed by them.
8. I am able to understand and respond sensitively to my partner's feelings.
9. I do a decent job balancing my need for intimacy with my need for achievement and success.
10. When I get stressed, I feel comfortable seeking comfort from my partner and close friends.

Once you have finished the survey, count your circled numbers under each section. The section that has the most circled numbers reflects your attachment style listed below.

- Attachment Style A = **Avoidant** attachment style
- Attachment Style B = **Anxious** (or Disorganized) attachment style
- Attachment Style C = **Fearful** (or Ambivalent) attachment style
- Attachment Style D = **Secure** attachment style

(Used by permission from Dr. Joshua Straub and Dr. Tim Clinton. Obtained from their book *God Attachment*.)

References

http://africa-facts.org/african-last-names/. *150 Unique and Most Common African Last Names*. Retrieved February 5, 2017.

http://www.nbcnews.com/id/39993685/ns/health-womens health/t/blacks-struggle-percent-unwed-mothers-rate/#. WFLzx8sm59A. Washington, Jesse. 11/2010. *Blacks Struggle With 72 Percent Unwed Mother Rate*. Retrieved December 15, 2016.

http://www.cdc.gov/injury/wisqars/index.html. Centers for Disease Control and Prevention (CDCP). (2013), (2011). Web-based Injury Statistics Query and Reporting System (WISQARS) [Online]. National Center for Injury Prevention and Control, CDC.

https://www.cdc.gov/nchs/fastats/unmarried-childbearing.htm. Center for Disease Control and Prevention. (2017). *Unmarried childbearing*. January 17. Retrieved November 17, 2017.

http://www.christianitytoday.com/edstetzer/2018/january/churchs-response-to-opioid-crisis-practical-tool-kit-for-fa.html. Stetzer, ed. *Christianity Today*. January 18, 2018. Retrieved January 19, 2018.

https://www.verywell.com/what-is-attachment-theory-2795337. Cherry, Kendra. *Bowlby and Ainsworth: What is Attachment Theory? The Importance of Early Emotional Bonds*. August 13, 2017. Retrieved October 25, 2017.

https://www.huffingtonpost.com/tim-wright/how-to-build-a-better-dad_b_3512878.html Wright, Tim. (2013). *How to "Build" a Better Dad.* Huffington Post. August 28. Retrieved October 27, 2017.

http://psychology.about.com/od/theoriesofpersonality/a/hierarchyneeds.htm. Cherry, Kendra. Retrieved October 31, 2015.

http://www.ibtimes.com/why-are-so-many-vietnamese-people-named-nguyen-1556359. Ghosh, Palash. 2/18/14. Retrieved, February 4, 2017.

http://specialtyretail.com/issue/2008/10/running-a-cart-or-kiosk/dealing-with-retail-theft/strategies_to_prevent_shoplifting_and_retail_theft/. Retrieved October 31, 2015.

http://www.samhsa.gov/data/sites/default/files/NSDUHmhfr2013/NSDUHmhfr2013.pdf. Substance Abuse and Mental Health Services Administration (SAMHSA), (2014). Results from the 2013 National Survey on Drug Use and Health: Mental Health Findings, NSDUH Series H-49, HHS Publication No. (SMA) 14-4887. Rockville, MD: Substance Abuse and Mental Health Services Available.

https://www.psychologistworld.com/developmental/attachment-theory.php. Retrieved December 10, 2016.

http://www.richmond.com/news/local/hanover/mechanicsville-local/opinion/stats-of-effects-in-broken-homes/article_ba88da2c-6af8-11e2-9f38-0019bb30f31a.html. *Richmond Times-Dispatch.* (2013). *Stats of Effects of Broken Homes.* January 30. Retrieved November 17, 2017.

https://www.statista.com/statistics/264810/number-of-monthly-active-facebook-users-worldwide/. Retrieved December 7, 2017.

https://www.thriveglobal.com/stories/16020-4-questions-we-unconsciously-ask-near-constantly. Schafler, Katherine. (2017). *How to Change Your Life in One Second Flat.* Retrieved November 15, 2017.

Ainsworth, M. D. S., and J. Bowlby. (1991). "An ethological approach to personality development." *American Psychologist* 46, 331–341.

Axelrod, Alan. (1997). *International Encyclopedia of Secret Societies and Fraternal Orders.* New York: Facts on File Publishers.

Barrett, David V. (1999). *Secret Societies: From the Ancient and Arcane to the Modern and Clandestine.* London: Blandford Publishers.

Beattie, Melody. (1992). *Codependent No More: How To Stop Controlling Others and Start Caring for Yourself.* Center City, MN: Hazelton Educational Materials.

Blackburn, Bill. (1982). *What You Should Know About Suicide.* Waco, TX: Word Books.

Bowen, Murray. (1974). "Toward the Differentiation of Self in One's Family of Origin." *Family Therapy in Clinical Practice.* Reprint. Lanham, MD: Rowman and Littlefield (published 2004), 529–547.

Bowlby, J. (1946). *Forty-Four Juvenile Thieves: Their Character and Home-Life.* 2nd ed. London: Bailliere, Tindall and Cox.

Bowlby, J. (1951). "Maternal care and mental health." *World Health Organization Monograph* serial no. 2.

Bretherton, Inge. (1922). "The origins of attachment theory: John Bowlby and Mary Ainsworth." *Developmental Psychology* 28, 759–775.

Bretherton, I., and K. A. Munholland. (1999). "Internal Working Models in Attachment Relationships: A Construct Revisited." *Handbook of Attachment: Theory, Research, and Clinical Applications.* J. Cassidy and P. R. Shaver, eds. New York: Guilford Press.

Brewer, Marilyn B. (1999). "The Psychology of Prejudice: Ingroup Love and Outgroup Hate?" *Journal of Social Issues* 55(3): 429–444. Doi101111/00224537.00126.

Cahn, Jonathan. (2016). *The Book of Mysteries*. Lake Mary, FL: Front Line/Charisma House Book Group.

Chironna, Mark. (2015). Facebook post. Retrieved 2015.

Clinton, Tim, and Gary Sibcy. (2006). *Why you do the things you do: the secret to healthy relationships*. Nashville, TN: Thomas Nelson.

Clinton, Tim, and Joshua Straub. (2010). *God Attachment: why you believe, act, and feel the way you do about God*. New York: Howard Books.

Cohen, Lisa J. (2011). *The Handy Psychology Answer Book*. (308–314; 433–434). Canton, MI: Visible Ink Press

Crabb, Larry (2005). *Connecting: healing for ourselves and our relationships*. Nashville, TN: Thomas Nelson.

Diagnostic and Statistical Manual of Mental Disorders, Fifth Edition (DSM-5). (2013). Washington, DC: American Psychiatric Publishing.

Federal Bureau of Investigation. (2011). *2011 National Gang Threat Assessment—Emerging Trends*. http://www.fbi.gov/stats-services/publications/2011-national-gang-threat-assessment. Accessed November 20, 2017.

Fenelon. (1992). *The Seeking heart*. Jacksonville, FL: Seed Sowing Publishing.

Frankl, Victor. (2014). *Man's Search for Meaning*. Beacon Press. Boston, MA.

Hetherington, E. M. (2005). "Divorce and the adjustment of children." *Pediatrics in Review* 26(5): 163–169.

Johnson, Sue, and Kenneth Sanderfer. (2016). *Created for connection*. New York: Little, Brown.

Kanter, J. (2007). John Bowlby, Interview with Dr. Milton Senn. *Beyond the Couch: The Online Journal of the American Association for Psychoanalysis in Clinical Social Work*, issue 2. Retrieved from: http://www.beyondthecouch.org/1207/bowlby_int.htm.

Kiefer, Heather Mason. (2004). "Empty Seats: Fewer Families Eat Together." Gallup, Religion and Social Trends. January 20. http://www.gallup.com/poll/10336/empty-seats-fewer-families-eat-together.aspx. retrieved July 9, 2017.

Kindlon, Dan, and Michael Thompson. (2000). *Raising Cain: Protecting the Emotional Life of Boys*. New York: Ballantine Books.

Krohn, Franklin B., and Zoe Bogan. (2001). "The Effects Absent Fathers Have on Female Development and College Attendance." *College Student Journal* 2001. Bnet. Web. 18 February 2010. http://findarticles.com/p/articles/mi_m0FCR/is_4_35/ai_84017196/pg_2/?tag=conten; col1.

Lawhorne, Cheryl, and Don Philpott. (2010). *Combat-Related Traumatic Brain Injury and PTSD: A Resource Recovery Guide*. Lanham, MD: Government Institutes.

Maslow, Abraham. (1970). *Motivation and Personality*. 2nd edition. New York: Harper and Row.

McDowell, Josh. (1996). *The Father Connection*. Nashville, TN: Broadman and Holman.

McGuinness, Teena M., PhD., APRN-BC. (2006). "Marriage, divorce, and children." *Journal of Psychosocial Nursing and Mental Health Services*, 44(2): 17–20. Retrieved from http://search.proquest.com/docview/225539268?accountid=12085.

McLeod, S. A. (2009). *Attachment Theory*. www.simplypsychology.org/attachment.html. Retrieved December 10, 2016.

Mellody, Pia. (2003). *Facing Codependence: What it is, Where it Comes from, How it Sabotages Our Lives*. New York: HarperCollins

Mercer, J. (2006). *Understanding Attachment*. Westport, CT: Praeger.

Minuchin, Salvador. (1974). *Families and Family Therapy*. Boston: Harvard University Press.

Nehrbass, Daniel. (2017). How To Develop an Effective Support Ministry for Adoptive and Foster Parents. A chapter in the book, *The Struggle is Real: How to Care for Mental and Relational Health Needs in the Church*. Edited by Timothy Clinton and Jared Pingleton. WestBow Press. Bloomington, IN.

Newman, Heather, RN. (2013). "Mental Health Matters: The Power of Bullying." *Centra Mental Health Services* 27(3) September.

Nichols, M. (2010). *Family Therapy, Concepts and Methods*. 9th ed. New York: Prentice Hall.

Nouwen, Henri, and Jeff Imbach, eds. (2005). *Words of Hope and Healing: 99 sayings by Henri Nouwen*. New City Press of the Focolare.

Oxford American College Dictionary. (2002). New York: G. P. Putnam's Sons.

Pitts, Quint. 2016. *Celebrating Recovery with our Veterans*. Celebrate recovery, Welcome Home Division. November 14. http://pastors. com/celebrating-recovery-with-our-veterans/. Retrieved May 2, 2017.

Resnick, Michael D., et al. (1997). *Protecting Adolescents from Harm: Findings from the National Longitudinal Study of Adolescent Health*. JAMA 278(10), September 10.

Rihbany, Abraham Mitrie. (1916). *The Syrian Christ*. Boston: Houghton Mifflin.

Rogers, C. (1961). *On Becoming a Person: A Therapist's View of Psychotherapy*. Boston: Houghton Mifflin.

Root, Andrew. (2010). *Youth, family, culture: Children of divorce*. Grand Rapids, MI: Baker. Retrieved from http://site.ebrary.com.ezproxy. liberty.edu:2048/lib/liberty/docDetail.action?docID=10659. 979.

Rutter, M. (1995). "Clinical Implications of Attachment Concepts: Retrospect and Prospect." *Journal of Child Psychology and Psychiatry* 36(4): 549–571.

Seligman, Linda. (2004). *Diagnosis and Treatment Planning in Counseling.* New York: Kluwer Academic.

Skoglund, Elizabeth. (1976). *Loneliness.* Downers Grove, IL: InterVarsity Press.

Steakley, K. (2008). *Child of Divorce, Child of God: a Journey of Hope and Healing.* Downers Grove, IL: InterVarsity Press.

Stine, Crystal. (2017). *Craving for Connection: 30 Challenges for Real-Life Engagement.* Nashville, TN: B and H Publishing Group.

Strohscheim, L. (2005). "Parental divorce and child mental health trajectories." *Journal of Marriage and Family* 67(5): 1286–1300. Retrieved from http://www.jstor.org/stable/3600313

Subby, Robert. (1984). "Inside the Chemical Dependent Marriage: Denial and Manipulation." *Co-Dependency, An Emerging Issue.* Hollywood, FL: Health Communications.

Teyber, E. (2001). *Helping Children Cope with Divorce.* San Francisco: Jossey-Bass.

Thoreau, Henry David. 2017. *Walden.* Originally published in 1854. Huntington, WV: Empire Books.

Tyre, Peg. (2006). "The Trouble With Boys." January 30. *Newsweek.*

Van Dijken, S. (1998). *John Bowlby: His Early Life: A Biographical Journey into the Roots of Attachment Theory.* London: Free Association Books.

Vanier, Jean. (1989), (2003). *Community and Growth.* New York: Paulist Press.

Vitz, C. (1977/1994). *Psychology as Religion: The Cult of Self-Worship.* 2nd ed. Grand Rapids, MI: William B. Eerdmans.

Waite, Linda J., and Maggie Gallagher. (2001). *The Case for Marriage: Why Married People are Happier, Healthier, and Better off Financially.* New York: Random House.

Waite, Linda J., and Maggie Gallagher. (2000). *The Case for Marriage: Why Married People Are Happier, Healthier, and Better Off Financially.* New York: Doubleday.

Welch, Edward T. (1997). When people are big and God is small. Phillipsburg, NJ: Presbyterian and Reformed Publishing.

Wight, Fred H. (1953). *Manners and Customs of Bible Lands.* Chicago: Moody Press.

Wilson, Chris M., and Andrew J. Oswald. (2005). "How Does Marriage Affect Physical and Psychological Health? A Survey of the Longitudinal Evidence." *Institute for Study of Labor.* Study Paper 1619. Bonn, Germany: Institute for the Story of Labor. May.

Yust, K., B. Hyde, and C. Ota. (2010). "Cyber Spirituality: Facebook, Twitter, and the adolescent quest for Connection." *International Journal of Children's Spirituality* 15(4): 291–293.

Zimbardo, Philip, and Nikita D. Coulombe. (2012). *The Demise of Guys: Why Boys Are Struggling and What We Can Do About It.* Amazon Digital Services.

About the Author

⌒

Christian counselor Dr. Robert B. Shaw Jr. is a Licensed Clinical Mental Health Counselor and Supervisor, dually licensed in Virginia and North Carolina. He is also an ordained minister, serving as a youth pastor, Christian education director, adult education director, musician, and executive pastor in churches in New Jersey, Colorado, Maryland, and in North Carolina, for over twenty-five years. He has also been a middle school and high school teacher and athletic coach in both the public and private school environments. Dr. Shaw has spent several years counseling in church settings and community agencies and counseling military personnel and their families near Ft. Bragg, North Carolina. He also ministers regularly in the Philippines. He specializes in trauma related issues; addictions; and victims of abuse, depression, anxiety disorders, life adjustment issues, loss and grief, counseling church leaders and pastors, adolescents, and adults. Dr. Shaw's is a unique prophetic voice in the kingdom caring for hurting people, and he serves as an adjunct professor for a Christian university, an author, and a sought-after conference speaker. Dr. Shaw has a Bachelor of Arts degree in religious studies from Wagner College, New York and a Master of Divinity degree from Christian

International Theological School, Florida. He also has a Master of Arts in professional counseling from Liberty University, Virginia and a Doctor of Ministry degree in formational counseling, a practical theology, from Ashland Theological Seminary, Ohio. He is a member of the American Association of Christian Counseling. Dr. Shaw enjoys running, sports, the beach, and spending time with friends and family.

Printed in the United States
by Baker & Taylor Publisher Services